TeeCee's 'Army Odes'

An illustrated collection of verses relating to the life and times of a REME soldier, both at the Arborfield Army Apprentice School and in the Regular Army.

By Tony Church

TeeCee's 'Army Odes'

By Tony Church

First Edition

Written and Compiled by Tony Church
Copyright ©2017 Tony Church

The moral rights of the author have been asserted. All rights reserved. No part of this publication may be reproduced, stored in a retrieval system or transmitted in any form or by any means, electronic, mechanical or otherwise without the written permission of the Publisher

ISBN Number: 978-0-244-31672-3

Design and Typesetting by David Schofield
Printed worldwide by Lulu.com

About the Author

Tony Church (Nom de Plume "TeeCee")

Born in Kingston upon Hull in April 1939.

Enlisted in The Army Apprentices in February1955 (55A) serving a three year apprenticeship at the Army Apprentices School at Arborfield, Berkshire, leaving as A/Drum Major of the School pipe band.

Served in the Royal Electrical and Mechanical Engineers (REME) for nine years in U/K, Cyprus and Aden, returning to civilian life in April1966.

Spent the remainder of working life in the Materials Handling Industry, in selling, maintenance and repair of Forklift Trucks.

Now retired, living in Titchfield, Hants, and still playing the drums in The Army Apprentices Pipes And Drums.
(TAAPAD)

In his own words …..

"I like to write poetry, or actually, verse, I prefer it to rhyme, (my
priority first.)
Real poets write in blank verse, some really highbrow, but I just
don't seem to get it, somehow.
Maybe my lifestyle has something to do with this flaw, I am certainly

somebody who
Will tap my feet merrily if I am given a lively and rhythmic tuneful
composition,
Which probably is why I do play the drums, and have, all my lifetime,
so that's where it comes
From, I guess, and I'm stuck with this failing of mine, so it's just a
thing to which I have to resign.

So, "Poet", I am not, let me make that plain, but "Wordsmith", I
like, it somehow retains
The aptness of setting words in such a way that they harmonise tidily,
always conveyed
In a manner which entertains, informs, maybe, but above all, is set
out to read pleasantly;
I guess that I will never equal Shakespeare, Alfred Tennyson yet,
though I might just come near
To that legendary Scot of McGonnigal fame – ah yes - the desire to be
linked with that name!
The name that resounds down the annals of time, a unique style coupled
with wit so sublime!

But there I go, dreaming of wide recognition when I should be content
with the humble ambition
Of writing this deathless stuff at my own leisure, and if in

the
writing there is derived pleasure
Or some message that I attempt to convey, then I will be satisfied if in my way,
I have given some interest, though albeit brief, in the written word,
which we read, in the belief
That the English language is still here to stay, despite all those
texts that are common today!
So all of you 'Wordsmiths', 'Muses' or 'Poets' keep up the good work
and let everyone know it!"

Part One: Junior Solders – 'Boys School'

Ode		Page
1	Army Apprentice School Badge	1
2	Boys School	3
3	Army Apprentice School	7
4	A Day in the Life of a JEEP	10
5	The 'Arborfield Slide'	14
6	The Barber	16
7	Bravo Company	17
8	The Drill Pig	18
9	The Drum Major	20
10	The RSM	23
11	The School Bands	25
12	Trade Training	28
13	Trades	31
14	The Firework Factory	33
15	Bull	35
16	Cheer Up	38
17	Christmas	39
18	Company Orders	41
19	Food (These Foolish Things)	43
20	Free Sunday	45
21	Guards Brigade Permanent Staff	47
22	Guards Sergeant Majors	48
23	Jankers	50
24	Joining Up	54
25	Our Fred	57
26	Reveille	59

27	Rodeo	60
28	Room Jobs	62
29	Passing Out Parade	63
30	"Plates"	66
31	Stickman	67
32	Thanks for the memories	69
33	A.A.S. Memorial 2014	72
34	Goodbye Arborfield	74
35	Arborfield revisited	76
36	Boys No More	79
37	Fifty Names	81
38	Final Chapter	83
39	Final Curtain	85
40	Old Comrades	87
41	Friendship	88
42	Happy New Year	90
43	Last Parade	91
44	Our Legacy	93
45	Musical Memories	95
46	Old Boys – Old Soldiers	97
47	One Old Boy's Reunion	100
48	Our Glorious Past	102
49	Remembering	104
50	Reunion 2012 a New Experience	107
51	Reunion Ode	111
52	The Reds	113
53	Sixty Up!	115
54	Soya Sausages	117
55	Spirit	118

56	The Gates of Fate	120
57	The Ghosts	122
58	The Heavenly Battalion	124
59	The Highland Bagpipe	126
60	The Drummers	128
61	The Memorial	129
62	The Good Old Days (?)	131
63	The Piper's Requiem	133
64	The Roll Call	135
65	The Roll Call 2	135
66	Two Minutes	137
67	Us	139
68	We, of this Group	140
69	Whither "Boy's School"	142
70	Airs on a bed spring	144
71	Yet Another Goodbye	146

Part Two: Regular Army Life

Ode		Page
1	Arte et Marte	153
2	Aden	155
3	Barrack Room Humour	158
4	Bill Millin, The Making of a Legend	160
5	Bloggs Bogs	164
6	Bombers Moon	166
7	Chuff Charts	168
8	Comradeship	170
9	"ECE'S"	172
10	Epitaph for Afghanistan	173
11	Heroes	175
12	Home at Last	177
13	Lights Out, At Rest	179
14	Numbers and Initials	180
15	Old Soldier	182
16	Pegasus. Ancient and Modern	184
17	Rece Mechs	186
18	Red Arrows	188
19	Sand in my Shoes	191
20	Silent Valley	193
21	Silent Witnesses	195
22	Six-One-Seven Sqn. The Dam Busters.	197
23	REME - Soldier First	200
24	Soldiers who Fight	201
25	Stand Easy	203

26	The Final Sunset	204
27	The Likely Lads	205
27	A Soldiers Tale (21st Century Style	207
29	The Soldier	209
30	The Uniformed Engineer	211
31	Thoughts on being a Soldier	213
32	Three Statues	215
33	Watching and Waiting	217
34	Whither the Army now?	219
35	Winter	222
36	Army Wives	224
37	At the Cenotaph	226

Part One: Junior Solders – 'Boys School'

Army Apprentice School Badge

The spurred gearwheel of industry, for faith, a simple cross,
The torch of learning on crossed swords, above the words embossed.
 "Army Apprentices School " worn by young boys with pride
Preparing to be artisans to give aid and provide
Support to soldiers everywhere, with skills they learned well spent
Protecting comrades from effects of war's hostile intent.

Numbered in their thousands for three score years and more
They formed the solid backbone of the Army's Tradesmen's Corps.
Working in the background, away from fame and glory,
They quietly performed their role, an unassuming story
Of skill and dedication and commitment to their trade,
Without whom many feats of arms would never have been made.

So honour those who wore it in their youth for all to see,
Remembering those who paid the soldiers debt for victory,
It has faded into history's page, no more to glint and shine
On caps and collars brightly, reminding of the time
When these young boys grew up and took their place where they should be,
In the forefront of the British Army's place in history.

TeeCee

Boys School

"Boys School". What do you recall of the place?
Where time seemed to move at a lowly snails pace,
Just counting the days till you went off on leave,
To freedom; for some just a temporary reprieve
From the gypping and bullying, too scared to rebel
At that Lancejack who daily was giving you hell.

And the jankers and rodeo which you had incurred
For some minor infringement, considered absurd
By your average civilian with plain common sense,
But which plagued you and made your daily existence
A struggle to keep your morale more or less
Above misery, hunger and sheer helplessness.

Those endless room jobs, the repetitive chores
Of dusting the lampshades, or bumping the floors
With that to-and-fro motion which could drive you insane,
Yet you knew in the morning, you'd do it again
And again and again, until shining and gleaming,
While all that you had was backache, muscles screaming.

But that was just while you were back in your room,
Once out on the square then, the unnerving boom
And ear-splitting scream of some banshees from hell
Had you doubling around until you couldn't tell
Whether coming or going and surely you'd give
Anything for civilian life that you had lived.

And down in the workshops things weren't any better,
All that filing and sawing of metal to get a
Flat surface to scribe on and then make a hole

Which you filed out again, your ultimate goal
Was to fit yet another piece matching the figure
Of what you'd removed, as your blisters grew bigger.

Those three years passed slowly. No. Time didn't fly,
Interminable days dragged as they passed us by,
It seemed we were stuck in a time warp, stagnating,
Existing on six bob a week and debating
As to whether we'd spend it on Zebo or polish
Important decisions which gave us no solace.

At last the day came that we'd yearned for so long,
And the times we'd rehearsed this parade were now done,
We slow marched and wheeled to the tune "Auld Lang Syne",
Making silent self promise that this was the last time
That we'd never march on that square ever again,
Remembering the blisters, the noise and the rain.
Now, fast-forward five decades, and thoughts idly turn
To those days of your youth. Curiosity burns
In your mind, and you wonder just what happened to
All those room-mates who shared your life and you knew
Much better than anyone, even their Mothers,
For you shared a life so much closer than brothers.

And then you remember the great times you had,
All that joking and laughter, and feeling quite sad
That you had lost touch with the spirit you shared
And those friends who had meant so much to you and fared
Along with you, your life with its highs and its lows,
Looking out at you still from those faded photos.

You think of how great those old Christmases were
When the senior ranks, officers all gathered there
To serve up the best meal of the year without doubt,

Roast turkey or chicken, spuds and Brussels sprouts
Followed by mince pies and then Christmas pud,
And felt at that moment that life was so good.

And mornings when gathered to go off on leave,
With pockets crammed full of the money retrieved
From our credits, so flush with the cash that we'd earned,
Those fivers we had that now literally burned
The holes in our pockets, just waiting to spend
As we headed for home to our family and friends.

Yet when you arrived and met up with your mates,
They somehow seemed changed, it was just that innate
Feeling that something was missing you felt,
A sense that what you had, had faded to melt
Into past times now gone from recall, now estranged,
When in truth, they'd not altered, it was you who had changed.

Then it dawned on you slowly that life as you knew it
Was gone, and your new life as you traversed through it
Would hold far more interest than you had foreseen,
When you walked through those gates at the age of fifteen.
For as you learned, gaining experience then,
You had changed, unaware, turned from youths into men.

So look at it once again as the time passes,
And probably you'll feel the need to wear glasses,
While some may have lens with a quite rosy hue,
Others will never feel, as many do,
That our time spent at "Boys School" was not dissipated,
And our formative years there were not ever wasted.

TeeCee

Army Apprentice School

The names may come, the names may go, but 'Boy's School' is **the** one we know,
That place where we took our first steps to manhood, which we long have kept
And cherished in those secret parts, the private corners of our hearts,
A spot along a leafy lane midst countryside, where we all came
And nervously anticipated future trials that awaited.

It seems strange now with hindsight clear, just why, as we had volunteered
To "learn a trade" and "see the world", why was it that our stomachs curled
And twisted into painful knots at the prospect of our lot
In slavery for a lifetime then? Or so it seemed, our youth stolen
For bondage was our revelation - no time for tears, recrimination

Of course it wasn't like that long, and we soon realised we were wrong,
Our opening thoughts had been perverse, in practice, it was much much worse!
Adapting to our lowly station, we endured humiliation
That would break some lesser boys, so then we soon learned to deploy
Practices of lowly cunning when we detected trouble coming!

But then as time passed, in our turn, we were the ones who came to earn
The kudos of the senior boys; for all the privileges we enjoyed
Had been earned in those junior days, and in the various many ways

It taught us how to stay alive, to work out how to cope, survive,
And learn life's lesson's early on, long before we would have done
Had we returned to civil life, escaping regimental strife.

All else was really incidental. Yes, trades and drill were most essential
For our future progress too, but first we needed to get through
That heartbreak when we left our homes and families, intent to come
Into a military way of living, adapt to life quite unforgiving,
For we were merely naïve lads who'd mostly had our Mums and Dads
To help protect from life's hard knocks, wiped our noses, washed our socks,
Comforted when we were low, watching us from childhood grow.

We entered Boy's School as those boys, but left as men with certain poise
And confidence to face and take life's challenges, go on and make
Our own way by those lessons learned in early years, and, unconcerned
By setbacks found along the way, live those lessons day by day
That Boy's School burned into our souls, taught us to achieve our goals,
And fear no bully, braggart too, become known as a person who
Would fight for all things he thought right, looking to a future bright.

Though Boy's School may now be long gone, its values will still carry on
In those who had the very great good fortune to pass through those gates.
And now, with wisdom that time brings, we reminisce about those things

Which gave our lives a new direction with a genuine affection,
Regretting though, now it has gone, the benefits that could have come
To modern youth; how changed their fates if they could still pass through those gates.
TeeCee

A Day in the Life of a JEEP

Reveilles blast assaults your ears; you stumble from your pit,
All thoughts of sleep are left behind, while laying out your kit.
You've got an hour to get it all lined up, with time to spare,
Before the dreaded bugle call to muster on the square.

Down for breakfast, join the queue, then senior divs appear,
You're gypped again - the rotten swine! But keep mouth shut for fear
Of rough reprisals later on, it isn't worth a light,
Being a jeep's just not much fun, and you know it isn't right.

But that's the way it's always been, you know your time will come,
When it's your turn to be real mean, and they'll, in turn, play dumb.
Collect your greasy eggs and tea, you've got no time to eat,
Then time your exit to miss the "Plates!" And beat a swift retreat!

Back to the billet. Room jobs now, you're on 'bump centre deck.'
Mix Zebo with that orange wax, you mustn't miss a speck
Of dirt - you really break your back, to get that shine just right,
A pity though, it won't last long when the lads return tonight.

Time to get the clobber on, boxed denims, shirt and tie,

Jacket, get your beret straight, one inch above the eye,
Pull on your boots, check webbings right, -"Five minutes Before's "- the rule,
Late on Parade?   Not on your life! You learn FAST at this school!

Half an hour of square-bound joy then follows- what a bind!
The bellowing of soldier- boys, enough to blow your mind!
But wait! The day has just begun, there's a lot more yet to come,
Workshop training, followed by a long cross country run!

March to the workshops, grab your file, attack that lump of steel,
Scrape to and fro till blisters show, until the midday meal,
Get gypped again, but what the hell, you're too fed-up to care,
Back to your room, it's time to change for PT, don't despair,

Cross country runs are good for you, so say the PTI's
But no good arguing with those chaps, so under leaden skies,
You set off at a steady jog, and head down Hogwood Lane,
And sure enough, within a mile, it's pouring down with rain.

Returning, knackered, cold and wet, you stagger to your room,
Go to the shower, there to find no lights to pierce the gloom,
The water's cold, you just can't see to get yourself cleaned off,
It's all supposed to make you hard, but all you feel is, rough.

And when, at last, the day is done, you crawl back to your pit,
Your will to live just lingers on, although you'd like to quit,
So, ask yourself as night time falls," Is Civvy Street so good?"
"Would I go back to Civvy pay?" TOO BLOODY RIGHT I WOULD!"

TeeCee

The 'Arborfield Slide'

It's not in the drill book, you'll not find it there,
It's broken the heart of drill pigs on the square,
No matter how hard they all shouted and tried
To outlaw it, it lived on - the 'Arborfield Slide'.

Employed in the main when marching to class
Or moving from A to B - mostly en masse,
It was the special way of achieving the 'halt'
With flair and panache, a move to exalt.

On word of command as left foot passed the right,
The right boot stamped down, while the left dragged up tight
Against side of the left, as the right stamped once more,
With slight bend of the knee, all in total rapport.

To say it was frowned on by Permanent Staff
Was a large understatement, it quite drove them daft
With frustration and anger, and still, without doubt
Their efforts to forbid it all came to nowt.

And now, at the Old Boys reunions we see
That the Arborfield Slide's achieved longevity,
For, when on parade, and though decades have gone,
When the halt is called, the "Slide" still lives on!

TeeCee

The Barber

He sits his victim in the chair with grim determination,
Attacks the remnants of his hair without sophistication.
The buzz of shears, the howl of pain is music to his ears,
As scissors flash, the deed is done, ignores the groans and tears.
No social chat, no sly invite for "Something for the weekend"
Just brief brush down, whips off the cloth as to his task he bends.
Short back and sides, that's all he does, it is the army style,
And requests for "Just a trim" are met with a grim smile,
For if it shows outside the cap, it ends up on the floor,
And what's inside he gives short shrift, and you can be sure
That 'Style' is not a word in his vocabulary,
It's all or nowt, as he proceeds along with fiendish glee.
So hope's abandoned when you cross his threshold – it ain't funny,
He'll give an Aussie sheep shearer a good run for his money!

TeeCee

Bravo Company

If you've been to the pictures, I'll bet you've all seen
'The Red Badge of Courage', up on the big screen.
Or 'The Big Red One', though it's not generally known
That the colour selected was decided upon
Because of the fame of a great Company
At Arborfield Boys School – yes - Company "B"!

The red flash denoted the membership of
A chosen elite, elevated above
The mere ranks of squaddies not privileged to be
Chosen to reside in this aristocracy.
It was their misfortune to dwell in the shade
Of the best bunch of soldiers, ever seen on parade.

Yes, I know that there'll be those who just wouldn't agree,
And it's really quite reasonable, as some jealousy
Is bound to occur among those who were sent
To average Companies, and therefore hell bent
On venting frustration because they were not chosen,
And consequently complained, ten to the dozen.

But 'B' Company lads understand, and are sad
That some who can't make the grade, really get mad
And hot under the collar, proclaiming their loss,
(Though it's true to say that they don't give a toss!)
So never mind chaps, it's just one of life's jests,
In the presence of Class, there must be second best!

TeeCee

The Drill Pig

He stands and looks with great distaste at quivering Jeeps lined up, aghast
At what he sees. And casts his eyes towards the sky above, and sighs.
"Cor Blimey! Here we go again, attempt to turn boys into men?
I don't know why I bother – straight, this 'orrible lot are gonna hate
My guts before the day is done." and, pace stick raised, begins to run
His hapless victims round and round, Left turn! Right Turn!
Until the sound Of crunching boots has finally stilled his raging sadists soul, and filled
His heart with sated, savage joy, as he continues to destroy
Their individual self esteem, **and moulds them to a perfect team.**

This is the army's way, you see, of changing boys' thoughts drastically,
Each one had thought he was the best, superior to all the rest,
A cut above the common herd, but now he's realized it's absurd.
It bonds his pals in common cause, to help, encourage, for he knows
That they will do the same for him, when times are hard and things look grim.
So spare a thought for drill pigs too, they do the things they have to do,
For long term good in soldiers lives, so every one, in his way, strives

To keep the Army's good repute, enabling them to then recruit
More men and boys, who'll carry on tradition, that's so bravely won.

TeeCee

The Drum Major

You gaze at the assembled band. In solitary splendour, there, you stand.
The sword hangs heavy on your thigh, the dress chords, tassels, sashes lie
In great profusion on your chest, the gauntlets glow white, softly rest
Upon the Mace, all burnished bright, encrusted chain, reflecting light.

They wait; anticipate command, the Pipes and Drums and Military Band.
And in the rear, parading there, the Companies set to prepare
To march to their allotted place, rehearsed, and ready then to face
The approbation of the crowd, the Fathers, Mothers, Siblings, proud.

You turn about, become aware you're all alone, there's no-one there,

No serried ranks in front to guide your marching feet, or at the side
No markers there within your sight, you're in the lead, just get it right!
So, take deep breath, silent prayer, it's time to march on to the Square.

"Quick March!" You step out. Watch your pace, no need to dawdle or to race,
Don't make them step short, or outpace them, keep to a good, firm, steady rhythm.
The Bass Drum beat, the Snare Drum roll, the soaring Pipes invade your soul,
The measured swing of six-eight beat, transferring tempo to your feet.

You grip the Mace; flourish with style, but carefully listening all the while,
Prepared to signal change of tune, as planned before, in the Band Room.
And, constantly watching the line, to execute the turn on time,
Then, wheeling left, take up your place, facing the saluting dais.

You hold the Mace aloft, a sign to end the march, then realign
Yourself by turning right about, to face the band, hearing the shouts
Of NCOs as they take post. Then all is still, as the great host
Of people now upon the Square come to attention, waiting there.

That's how it goes; it's just the start of all parades, when you take part,
Behind the swank and glamour there, you're centre stage, so have a care
To get it right for all to see, and try to avoid the calamity,
The horrendous, ultimate disgrace, which happens if you drop the Mace!

TeeCee

The RSM

He strides, like God, upon the Square, there's apprehension in the air.
An awesome figure, carved in stone, he stands erect, aloof, alone.
The eagle eye surveys the scene, nostrils flare, and from between
His lips comes forth a strident roar. Hundreds flinch, and then, before
The next executive command, they, in expectation stand
Anticipating the loud blast, to propel them into fast
Reaction, and the moment when the expletive explodes again
Into their ears, they'll act as one, boots raise the dust – parade's begun!

With pace stick swirling to and fro, he marches them round, fast and slow.

Berating all who fail to match his standards, or, not up to scratch
With drill or dress, they'll pay the price, and in the future will think twice
Before they carelessly perform and face his wrath, endure the storm
Of his displeasure, loud and clear, extremely painful to the ear!
Yes, he's the Master of the Square and woe betide all those who dare
To desecrate the sacred ground, by slouching or playing around.
They'll find they're sweeping it all day, as punishment fits the crime, they say,
And learn the lesson taught to them - you don't mess with the RSM!

TeeCee

The School Bands

Lilting music fills the air, the Boys School bands are on the Square!
Rhythms dancing on the breeze, as marching feet stretch out to seize
And hold the beat in four-four time, while horns and trumpets, drums and chimes
Breathe life into the weary soul, raising spirits - that's their role,
To give that music added pep, and put spring into weary step.

Then, marching paused – inspection time – the skirl of pipes begins to climb
In slow, such slow, close harmony, the plaintive airs and melody
Rise over the assembled throng, soothing sounds that cause the songbirds
To cease their trills and hesitate, to compete with such a

thrilling, great
Uplifting sound that evokes in men, visions of a Scottish glen.

And, stepping off, they all combine to give a rousing, roaring, fine
Rendition of a well known air, as, playing, marching with great flair,
They pass the dais, straight as a die. Drum Majors, maces held on high
Salute - eyes right - and then proceed along the square to finally lead
Them off parade, their task complete. Now all that's heard is tramping feet.

But versatility is the norm, and the Military band is quite at home,
Playing dances, jazz, palm court, or tuneful sounds of any sort.
At functions grand or venues small, they'll persevere and give their all
In pursuit of the excellence that marks their sheer accomplishment.
They give the school good value too, their efforts great, achievements true.

The Pipe band also gets around, at village fetes they're often found,
And carnivals at summer tide, but on Burns Night they hit their stride.
With Haggis Pipings to attend, demand's so great, to avoid offence

They move around at double speed, toasting Rabbie, then they need
To move on to the next venue – another toast, or one, or two!

This really tends to slow them down, but not for shirking they're renowned,
They carry on so manfully that even if there's two or three
More places they must go to play before the finish of the day,
They'll valiantly consume the tot, then play until they've done the lot,
Then totter back to their cold beds, and on the morrow, nurse their heads!

But both the bands are at their best, on ceremonials that attest
To skills they learned while at the school, of discipline, and keeping cool
At all times under pressure, so, they'll play until it's time to go.
As "Sunset's last notes die away, remember these boys as they play,
These are not full time careers – it's just their hobby – for three years !

TeeCee

Trade Training

We joined the army as young boys, our aim, to learn a trade,
So, in the very early months, a foundation was laid
To make us useful with our hands, and learn to use the tools,
Gain expertise in basic skills, and learn about the rules
Of engineering theory, how to make ourselves proficient
At filing, sawing, blacksmithing, in short, to be efficient
So that, after our apprenticeship, as members of the Corps
We'd keep the reputation of the school, as always, to the fore.

To this end we toiled, perspired, to gain the skills we sought,
Endless chipping, filing lumps of metal, we were taught
That when, "up at the sharp end" no machines would be around,
These basic skills, acquired today, invaluable, would astound
And win the admiration of those relying on

Our expertise and aptitude for improvisation.
For basic skills such as we learned, could make the difference
Between success's great reward, or failure's consequence.

The blisters, cuts and bruises, the burns that we sustained,
Were marks of honour, borne with pride as manual skills we gained.
Whether in the blacksmith's shop, amidst the hot emissions,
Sweating, trying hard to beat hot steel into submission.
Among the smoke, the heat, and through the overpowering noise,
The hammers swung and anvils rung by keen and eager boys.
Or in the fitting shops where trade test work, so intricate,
Was laboured over in the quest to make it accurate.

At the end of workshop training, final tests had to be faced,
To show we'd mastered all the skills, and swiftly, as we raced
To beat the deadlines that our shrewd instructors had devised,
We filed and polished our test pieces, cunningly disguised
The odd *faux pas* - hoped to escape the ever seeing eye
Of the dreaded test inspector – it was always worth a try!
But futile. He'd seen all the tricks and wheezes they'd employed
O'er all the years, by thousands of young, devious, cunning boys.

Now, looking back through time, and with the knowledge that it brings,
We see, and can appreciate the very many things
That we were taught so *thoroughly,* with no expense in mind,
And *quality* the yardstick that applied, back at that time.

No time was wasted; we worked hard, instructors worked hard too,
Their dedication to their work, ensuring that those, who
Deserved success, should gain the goals which in the future lay.
We owe our heartfelt thanks to them, for showing us the way.

TeeCee

Trades

The trades we were taught were really quite fraught with the theory, not practice, I found,
The lads with the brains were the ones who most gained from these lessons on subjects profound.
So Telemechs, Radarmechs, Ecces and such, where the theory was all in the mind,
Meant hands didn't get hurt or covered in dirt, as the Fitters or VM's would find.

They'd sit in their chairs in the workshop from where air conditioners gently would blow,
While the Vehicle Mechs (A) would be toiling all day under great lumps of iron below.
Now the VM's and Fitters, you'd think would be bitter at this blatant trade segregation,
But they never mind, for in grease always find, inexplicably, great satisfaction.

For they spend all their time slaving, covered in grime, faces slippery with sweat and exhaustion,
While the chosen elite, smelling sweet and effete, look at diagrams seeking solution.
But the main satisfaction derives from the action of swinging a hammer precisely,
To know where to hit it, how hard it's permitted, a wallop or just to tap, lightly.

For Fitters, VM's, either (A), (B) or (C), are such macho men, muscular, hairy,
They work, never flag, always deep in the clag where it's only the levels that vary.

But when all's said and done, they are all part of one indispensable military Corps,
Without whom machines and mechanical means of armed conflict could not
go to war.
So here's to the tradesmen of all kinds, let's aid them to stay in the lead, good and trusty,
And fervently hope they'll continue to cope, with those tools that should never go rusty!
TeeCee

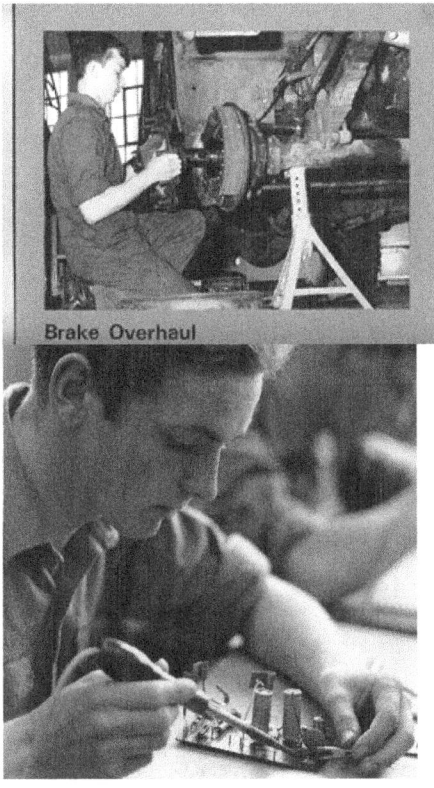
Brake Overhaul

The Firework Factory

In a back lane in Arborfield, long, long ago,
Stood a firework factory, right in the shadow
Of an Army Apprentices place, which was known
As a finishing school of worldwide renown.

Now this factory was mostly hidden by trees,
And the boys took no notice, too busy to see
What went on at the works, in fact they were bored,
There were things more important than what they had stored.

And, of course, they stored cordite, gunpowder and stuff,
Without it, the bangers would scarcely go, "Puff!"
And rockets would hardly be able to fly,
Roman Candles just wouldn't get into the sky.

So life was quite peaceful, with nothing much on,
When all of a sudden, a detonation,
Rocked the Spiders, the Cookhouse, the classrooms et al,
And a column of smoke covered all in its pall.

Not waiting for orders, some lads jumped the fence,
And twenty or so headed into the dense
Conflagration, the noise, the smoke and the heat,
Rolling out drums, though they hardly could breathe.

And when it was ended, the following day,
The National Press had this much to say:
"Boys from the neighbouring school were so brave,
Rolling out drums of gunpowder, to save
The lives of the workers, and in the end, won,

Everyone owes them, a heartfelt "Well done!"

The lads were nonplussed on hearing this news,
They'd reacted as trained, "Nothing special" they mused,
Though one of them was heard to say to his chums,
"Bloody Hell! So THAT's what was inside those drums!"

TeeCee

Bull

Of three years training constantly to learn a trade, efficiently,
And military training simultaneously, I reckon, in the end, that we
Spent in all, (industriously) at least nine months, toiling endlessly
To clean our kit and rooms, to be inspected so officiously
By those told by the powers-that-be, to watch our conduct carefully.

So expertise with iron and brush, with bumpers there to pull and push
Across the floor, till all shone bright, no speck of dirt shown up to blight
The pristine palace that we made, to put the others in the shade,
And earn ourselves the plaudits loud, of CSM's, to make us proud
Of all our efforts to excel, by months of practise, done so well.

The bucket, once so grey and dull, polished bright, reflecting all
The sunbeams chased through windows clean, and the lockers in between
Shining like the midday sun, aligned precisely, one by one.
Alongside beds and bed blocks smart, guaranteed to lift the heart
Of all who'd slaved to make it so, a truly grand, immaculate show.

And, as we stand there, dressed to kill, knife edge creases, sharper still
Than well honed blades, with belts so white, and boots with toecaps shining bright,
Gleaming buttons, all arrayed in perfect order, on parade.
Who would guess the stress and strain that we went through to finally gain
This spectacle of orderliness, immaculate in kit and dress?

The previous night, in midst of chaos, scenes of unbelievable pathos,
As twenty anxious, sweaty Jeeps, enough to make a grown man weep,
Queued up to press their best SD with just one iron, and desperately,
Impatiently, to get it done, insulting, barracking the one
Who, with brown paper, water, brush, endeavoured to placate the crush.

The smell of scorching filled the air, steam and swearing, moans and glares
As tramline creases came to light, so, cursing, tried to put it right.
And in the panic, big brown burn, with silver coin attempt to turn
It back into its normal hue, rubbing down the marks anew,
Then giving it a final press with paper brown, at last – success !

Yet, come the dawn, inspection time, those scenes have faded from the mind,
Everything is calm, and yet, this time next week you'll safely bet
That it'll be the same again - controlled panic - and it's plain

For all to see, no matter how you try to organize it, still somehow
It always ends up – you can guess - a muddled, never ending, mess !
TeeCee

Cheer Up

I suppose there are times when we all feel quite low,
And for ordinary blokes who have nowhere to go
To unload all their troublesome worries and fears,
Unable to find a considerate ear,
Life must seem at times to be too much to bear,
Lacking someone who is able to share
And sympathise, help, and listen a while,
Until all cares are banished, and able to smile.

But thankfully, that is the fate we evade,
For while we were busily learning a trade,
We also were weaving a bond, never broken,
Which tied us for life with a vow, quite unspoken,
That we would remain truly comrades of worth
To each other, even to the four corners of Earth,
So, like it or not, 'cos you're luckily numbered
Among Arborfield ex-boy's, you really are lumbered!

TeeCee

Christmas

Anticipation, you can feel it, hanging in the air,
The days to do are getting few, it's all too hard to bear.
That longed for day, when, laden down with credits, drawing near,
You're through the gates to liberty, full of Christmas cheer.

No drill, no workshop practice, far away from saw and file,
Just getting home and seeing friends and family for a while.
Letting your Mum make your bed, and helping you unpack,
Then meet your mates, so they can ask you, "When you going back?"

But not just now, there's still that Christmas dinner yet to eat,
Served up by smiling (!) Senior Ranks, a veritable treat!
The dances and the concerts, when the lads let down their hair,
(Yes, it wasn't long enough - figuratively speaking there!)

Then on that glorious morning, as "Reveille" splits the air,
The CSM, with rum-laced tea appears and starts to share
The "Gunfire" out among the lads, to warm them on their way,
Cracking jokes, indulging in benevolent survey.

And raise a glass to those whose Christmas wasn't meant to be,
Their lifetime's race now run, surrendering to mortality,
We'll miss them, but let's celebrate those boyhood ties, which bind,
Giving some comfort to those loved ones now left behind.

So now, to those who read these words, remembering it all,
You know how we enjoyed it then, and how we had a ball.
A Merry Christmas every one, wherever you may be,
To you and yours now, on this festive anniversary.

TeeCee

Company Orders

The lad stands by the Orderly room and contemplates his fate,
The Sergeant Major's voice of doom makes him anticipate
A longish stretch of punishment to make him mend his ways,
Which he'll find inconvenient (!) for seven or fourteen days.

So he removes his hat and belt, ('cos that's the way it's done)
Checks his dress, prepares himself for his retribution.
Then, crashing boots, through swinging doors, he's in with headlong rush,
While bellowing commands resound, then sudden, deadly hush.

Facing him, across the desk, the CO sits, and frowns,
While listening to the charge of his misdeed, as written down.
He speaks. "Well, what have you to say about this evil crime?
Can you give me one excuse, to mitigate your shame?"

The lad knows that it's futile to deny his delinquency,
And mutters,"No excuse Sir!" Prepares for ignominy.
He listens, captive audience, while the CO then expounds
How military discipline could ultimately break down.

If he should go unpunished, then anarchy would reign,
And spread out to the civil population, it would gain
Momentum, then eventually bring down the Government,
Then civil war would then ensue, caused by the discontent.

So given all this circumstance, his punishment would be
Confined to barracks for three days, ensuring then that he
Would learn a useful lesson, and an example made,

To others who were guilty of being late on parade!

The message contained in this verse is very plain to see,
That if you decide to sign on, and join the military,
You'll learn the phrase that all the squaddies long ago, had coined,
"If you can't a joke, old son, you shouldn't have bloody joined!"

TeeCee

Food (These Foolish Things)

Those squares of margarine afloat on water,
The scrambled eggs that we should really oughta
Have thrown in the bin, those inedible things,
With bromide filled brew.

The soya sausages that swam in gravy,
And greasy chips, stone cold all bent and wavy,
Fried bread burnt black and charred, we had it hard,
So painful to chew.

The dehydrated spuds we had to swallow,
Along with Yorkshire pudding, tough and hollow,
And, oh, those hard-boiled eggs, they were the dregs,
Solid through and through.

But we were growing lads and always starving,
So that whatever joint that they were carving,

We ate it all, large pieces and small,
In bits or in stew.

Yet we survived the food, went on to grow up,
Although a lot of it might make us throw up,
The hunger pangs still stay in memory today,
All our life through.

TeeCee

Free Sunday

You open one eye, surely something is wrong,
It's time to get up; you've been sleeping too long!
Why no loud bugle blast and no rough wake-up calls?
Where's the pace-stick that's thumping the barrack room walls?

And slowly, as drowsiness seeps from your brain,
The realization! - Free Sunday again!
No pressure, no need to prepare for parade,
Your Master – the clock- ignored, not obeyed!!

At least, for the rest of the day you are free
To do as you please, taking life easily.
What to do? Have a lie-in? Or stroll without haste
To the cookhouse for breakfast along with your mates?

The options seem endless, a luxury now,
Of choices to do as you will, so just how
Will you spend the remainder of this perfect day,
Free from commands that you have to obey?

It comes about every fourth Sunday, you may
Choose to idle around in the NAAFI all day,
Or go out to the town and blow all your pay,
Then return, feeling fragile, and less than OK!

In our youth this free day was the longed-for occasion
That was observed with much eager anticipation,
It freed us from bondage, though temporary,
Reminding us what it was like to be free.

And then, in years later, when called to the mind,
It underlined all those long days of hard grind,
And the value of freedom which many can't see
If they haven't experienced it's loss, as did we.

And its value, a thing on which spirit will thrive,
Is the right that no person should ever deprive
Of another, the birthright that mankind should hold
As so sacred, too priceless to ever be sold.
TeeCee

Guards Brigade Permanent Staff

We hated them, or thought we did, until time came to go,
For three long years, with gritted teeth, while marching to and fro
We'd thought of nothing but escape from strident, loud commands,
Unquestioning obedience to their endless demands.
Then gradually, towards the end, we see what they have done,
And slowly dawning in our minds the realization
That, disguised in the daily grind of all that army life,
We've grown up, turned from boys to men, prepared to face the strife
Of military service and the discipline required
To make a success of our chosen path, and – yes - inspired
By gentlemen, who came to teach us from The Guards Brigade,
Who, by their fine example, helped us also make the grade.
So, to all Guardsmen that we knew, their Regiments and ranks,
We give you all belatedly, our heartfelt, sincere thanks.

TeeCee

Guards Sergeant Majors

Into us the fear of God
They put, each time we daily trod
The sacrosanct patch that they owned,
That square, where we drilled, marched and groaned,
Even after all these years,
The memory still perseveres
Of strident roars, the loud commands,
The tramp of boots, the marching bands.

But we were boys then, young and green,
Not realising that between
Them, they were training us for life,

To face the trials and the strife
That we'd encounter on the way,
Preparing us then, for the day
When we'd eventually take their place
And like them,

TeeCee

Jankers

A/T O'Toole had been such a fool, going out when he should have been in.
So the very next day, with no undue delay, he was marched in to explain his sin.
The CO said, "O' Toole, while you're at this school, Standing Orders you have to obey."
"And to help you reform, seven days you'll perform, and confined to these barracks you'll stay."

O'Toole was so sad, it was hard for the lad to watch all his mates go to town,
While he had to work - he felt a right berk – peeling spuds till his fingers wore down.
And not only that, he had also to start getting kit bulled for evening parade,
Best SD to press, boots, belt, and then dress, attention to detail was paid.

For he knew, if he failed, he would then be assailed by the Orderly Sergeants great wrath,
And the following day, the price he would pay, on another charge, and that is tough.
For the cycle'd begin, the chances to sin while on Jankers, they would multiply,
So a seven day stint could become in an inst't, a fortnight or worse, could apply.

Therefore, duly at nine, he stands in the line of Defaulters, so nervous and glum,
While the Sergeant, so slow, inspects the first row, as he's

waiting for his turn to come.
The Sarge, with a frown, eyes him up and then down, and turns on his heel, walks away.
Then O'Toole grits his teeth, breathes a sigh of relief, he's survived for yet one more day.

The following dawn, O'Toole was forlorn at the prospect of six days to do,
All that bulling and beezing, a prospect displeasing, at the thought, his despondency grew.
So, up at Reveille, his courage he rallied, for he had an appointment with Fred,
And if he was late, such a terrible fate of more days, which filled him with dread.

Then, down to parade, with the others, he made his weary way to the Guardroom,
What jobs would he do? The Cookhouse, he knew, would be spuds again, peeling till noon.
But he thought he'd got lucky, a job not so mucky, he pulled QM's detail – that's good!
Inside, in the warm and the dry, he would try to filch items of kit if he could.

With his loot in his pocket, he knew he could flog it, when back to the Spider he went,
Selling ill-gotten gains, he would then take great pains to profit from his punishment.
But alas and alack, when reporting back to the QM's department, he found
That instead of work cushy, with whitewash and brush, he was shown a dirty great mound

It was coal in the yard, and the going was hard, but "coal has

to be whitewashed", it states,
To stop boys thieving the coal, and then heaving it all, over the fence to their mates.
Who, back at the Spider, then sat down beside the stove, stoking away till it glowed.
But the coal that was nicked, left a black mark, when picked, and the crime then quite
obviously showed!

So O'Toole learned a lesson, it's no use just guessing that jobs can be doddles, no fear!
To make such assumption shows sheer lack of gumption, as he found, while whitewashing the gear.
He thought that he'd cracked it, when he attracted the QM job, and so he laughed,
Forgetting that QM's activities ranged wide, from cushy, to downright hard graft!

The worst time he'd spend was at the weekend, the Saturday film in Camp Hall,
While he polished the brass and mowed all the grass, he could hear the lads having a ball.
And so, as the days of his time slipped away, as he tried to avoid further strife,
Released at the end, he vowed not to offend ever again in his life !

And so it goes on, Jankers never was fun, it's a punishment one must avoid,
But to give it wide berth, it never is worth to get those placed above you, annoyed.
Or you'll live to regret it, and they won't forget it, so humour them, make them feel good
So creep if you have to, although you won't want to, it's

better than peeling those spuds!
TeeCee

Joining Up

Nervous, apprehensive, seeing those imposing gates,
Wondering what lies in store, what future trials await;
Wanting to turn back, return again from whence we came,
Wishing we had never read recruiting posters claims.

But much too late we stand, confronting stark reality,
That we're committed to a life we entered voluntarily,
But, hiding grave foreboding, we put all our doubts aside,
And entered, all determined to take life in our stride.

That was the start of our careers so many years ago,
When all was sunny happy days,(or we recall it so,)
And we forget the first few days, bewildered, dazed and lost,
While trying to adjust to this New World, this line we crossed.

For now our past is done, forgotten- just a memory,
As we prepare to join this new, extended family,
Presently relinquishing our ties to dads and mothers,
Exchanging them for hundreds of assorted newfound brothers.

Though in those first few hours, still feeling empty and alone,
Existing in an alien world, just wishing we were home,
We're learning a first lesson very quickly, short and sweet,
Which is brought home to us, in short - to stand on our two feet.

No parents to protect us nor to shield us when we fail
To do what is required, no matter how we weep and wail,

We're masters of our future now, and we will stand or fall
By our own actions from this day, throughout life's fits and squalls.

And on that first night, laid in an unfamiliar, strange, cold bed,
Listening to muffled sobs and quiet teardrops shed,
As pangs of homesickness strike home to many youngsters there,
We start to grow up from this time, although not yet aware.

And this is how we differed from our pals in Civvy Street
Thrust into a grown-up world, our childhood incomplete,
We learned quite quickly to survive, mature more swiftly then,
Necessitating major change as we turned into men.

There were some boys who failed to change, who could not readjust,
But really not surprising when we look at the robust
Life that we were thrown into, the complete transformation
That we were called to undertake in our chosen vocation.

Now, with the gift of hindsight, looking back at times long past,
We see how these things shaped our lives, and showing the contrasts
With how a different path chosen would alter our life's course,
But all in all I think that we could have done a whole lot worse!

TeeCee

Our Fred

He was five feet three in his socks, I suppose,
With a small black moustache just under his nose,
Three chevrons affixed to his upper sleeve,
With a red and black armband, lead one to perceive
That this was the guardian of the main gate,
The one to avoid, if getting in late
From a night on the town, or just slightly drunk,
If he was on duty you knew you were sunk.

No drainpipe trousers passed his eagle eye,
Without remonstration, and if one were to try
To argue that these were okay, try to fool
This veteran soldier, out came the rule,
Then the cry, "Fifteen inches!" assaulted your ears,
And you knew it was hopeless, for over the years
He'd honed to perfection all of the ploys
That had been tried on, by hundreds of boys.

This wily old soldier ran a guesthouse,
Full board and lodging, and certain to rouse
The guests from their slumbers, at no extra cost,
Provided that they actively humoured their host
By helping with housework, and some minor chores,
With verbal encouragement, in shape of roars
Of derision, to turn the air blue,
Till all within sparkled, and glistened like new.

Maestro of the fire pump, he tried to show those
Who were on fire picquet the right way to hose
Down an inferno, and be able to get
Personnel out of danger, but he often got wet

Due to some inexperienced, ham fisted Jeep
Who'd pull the wrong handle, or fail to keep
To his detailed instruction, so in the end that,
He'd vent his frustration and jump on his hat!

His immaculate garden was his pride and joy,
But weeding and digging would always annoy
His guests, who, in fits of bad temper ensured
That seeds, when grown up, spelt out words that were rude!
When his sole means of transport, his trusty old bike,
Needing refurbishing, he sought to strike
A bargain with one guest, who, armed with paint pot,
Painted frame, tyres and saddle – the whole blooming lot!

He wasn't amused, I think it's fair to say,
And his invective, impressive, was heard far away,
As the guest, with demeanour so innocent then,
Saw that his sense of humour had somehow worn thin,
So in self preservation, seeing thunderous frown,
He legged it quite smartly till things had calmed down!
But our hero found out that he hadn't impressed,
When he found that he'd do extra time as a guest!

He was certainly not the most popular chap,
His duties precluded him being just that,
Though for ten years he jealously guarded that gate,
Fulfilling his duties, ignoring the hate
And resentment that always accompanied his task.
Never to have the occasion to bask
In the warm glow of friendship of lads in his charge
He'll not be forgotten, our Rifle Corps Sarge!
TeeCee

Reveille

Sweet Dreams. You lie, warm, far away
From toil and turmoil, a world so grey.
Wrapped in slumber, on sleep's wings
Your mind divorced from worldly things.

Then faint sound, breaking through the veil,
And growing louder, urgent, hails
The consciousness awake, to hear
The bugle calling, loud and clear.

Then, with a crash, the door swings wide,
A shadowy figure looks inside,
And flicks the switch, lights come alive,
The Orderly Sgt has arrived!

He murmurs greetings, asks so nice,
If we slept well, and, would a slice
Of toast be wanted with the tea
He's brought in so considerately?

Like Hell he does! He clatters in,
Bangs the lockers - what a din!
"Off Cocks, On Socks!" you hear the cry,
You won't sleep now, don't even try!

So put your feet down on the floor,
Get washing kit, head for the door
Down for a shave, ignore the pain,
Another day is here again!

TeeCee

Rodeo

(Extra weekend drill – punishment for minor transgressions)

Saturday lunchtime, Oh what bliss! Flaked right out, but Oh, what's this?
You've been a naughty boy it seems, and far from play, you know it means
That you'll be out, upon the square, in best SD, in suns hot glare,
Drilling for an hour or so, while all your mates get set to go
Out on the town to paint it red, while you're just marking time instead.

So heave a sigh, put on brave face, and best SD, best boots and lace
Them up, put on that belt, more depressed you've never felt.
If only you'd got out of bed the other day, than, instead,
Turned over for some extra kip, and given the duty sarge some lip,
At which point, he invited you to join the Company Orders queue!

So now the time's come to parade, you steel yourself for the tirade
Of Orderly Sergeants raucous shouts, as, left turn, right turn, turn about,
You don't know if you're coming or going, just keep on blindly following
The guy in front, don't make mistakes, ignore the heat and the aches
Of ankles, knees, calves and toes, just do everything that he does.

And now, at last, the end is near, "Dismiss!" is all you want to hear,
The sweat is running in your eyes, and, with all the other guys,
You've had enough, crime never pays, you've seen the error of your ways,
No way will you do this again, for one small slip, an hour of pain.
It's a game for cowboys to be won, but for squaddies – Rodeo's no fun!

TeeCee

Room Jobs

Who's on outside area and bumping centre deck?
Sergeant Major's coming round, we'll get it in the neck
If lampshades are still dusty, or bogs not shining bright,
And windows not immaculate we'll all be in the sh*te!

The grass is far too long, and now it's showing all the signs
Of needing us to get down on our knees with eating irons
And prune it so it's short enough to meet with his approval,
But KFS is not the best means to effect removal!

That bucket's lost the shine it had at CO's last inspection,
So get the brasso out, restore its previous perfection.
Shift the beds across, then ride the bumper to and fro,
Until the floorboards gleam and shine with incandescent glow.

And then at last with room jobs done, time for some relaxation,
At least that would be usually the normal expectation,
But this was Boys School, where our youth was long ago purloined,
They said, "If you can't take a joke, you shouldn't have bloody joined!"

For life was one long challenge there, you didn't hang about,
You took it in your stride, and learned to share the hardship out,
But one thing was consistent, keeping you at all times wearied,
You were permanently in the clag, only the level varied!

Passing Out Parade

The chairs lined up around the square, parents, siblings, girlfriends there,
Proudly wait expectantly for offspring to parade and see
The youngster who'd left home so green, to spread his wings, so eager, keen,
Mature into a fine young man, with back so straight, and fitter than
He'd ever been in days long past - a transformation, oh so vast!
They scarcely recognized the chap, immaculate, from toe to cap.

And as, so eagerly, they wait, a silence falls, then suddenly a great
Swell of sound invades the air, distantly, beyond the square.
Martial music, Pipes and Drums, diminished first, but nearer comes,
And growing louder with each beat, till the distant, marching fee

In a perfect, synchronized ballet, appear, and smartly make their way
To take their stations, (oft rehearsed, on wintry mornings till well versed!)

The bands wheel left and takes their post, playing till the boys, at last
Are then in place, by Company. There in front, conspicuously,
Stand erect the senior men, no longer boys, and here again
Together for the last parade, as is their due, a farewell paid
By all who'll follow in their wake, examples of what they can make
Of their young lives while at the school, if they just observe the rules.

Inspection time, and while the Brass perambulate, and slowly pass
The tiered ranks, so smart, so still, the sound of music starts to fill
The air with haunting melodies, as Pipes and Drums perform, then cease
As Brass and Reed take up the role, quietly play to soothe the soul.
A lull, a pause in ceremony, time for senior men, maybe,
To think a while on previous years, nostalgic thoughts, the laughs, the fears.

But now it all springs into life, the hoarse commands, sharp as a knife
Galvanise the waiting throng, as orders are obeyed as one.
The march past now, extended line, the bass drum beating in slow time,
As gleaming ranks pass by the dais. The "Eyes Right!" shout, and every face
Snaps round to proudly gaze upon the decorated chest of one
Whose rank entitles him to stand, saluting all, in manner grand.

Then change to quick time, arms now swing, pipes are skirling, chanters sing,
As ruler-straight ranks, heads held high, raise the dust as they march by.
White buckskin belts gleam in the sun, polished boots and buckles shone
To burnished lustre bright, a truly great, impressive sight
That one won't easily forget, a really grand occasion, yet,
One that's tinged with sadness too, as men move on to pastures new.

And finally, the pass out starts, the bass drum throbs, and in the hearts
Of all who watch the closing scene, good fortune wished, as now between
The slowly closing gates they pass, symbolizing now at last,
The time they've spent here now is done, the next phase of their life begun.
And as they cheer, and caps fly high, their faces turned up to the sky,
In years to come, when in times thrall, this day, fondly, they will recall.

TeeCee

"Plates"

It always seemed to be my fate to be the one who caught the "Plates!"
No matter how I tried to sneak out unobserved I'd hear that shriek
Triumphant, ringing in my ears confirming yet again my fears
That someone somewhere had a grudge, and seemingly I'd never judge
Time opportune when I could slink out of the room, and leave that sink
To someone else just for a change, at least, till I was out of range!

But time moves on, and when I earned two tapes, it then became my turn
To sit back, scrutinise and glower – oh, the utter, glorious power
I came to wield and give free reign! They sidled, dodged and tried in vain
To flee, escape by wit and guile from carrying evil, greasy piles
Of porcelain into the wash with stale, caked bits of squaddy nosh,
Through stacks of tins in glorious muddle, trying to avoid the puddles.

Although, in truth there wasn't much we wouldn't throw away or touch
With doubtful and suspicious notion; all we wanted was our portion
Of the grub which came our way, we really lived throughout each day,
Just dreaming of the next big spread, and salivating, looked ahead
To juicy steaks with sticky buns, and "Plates" was just a risk to run
In pursuit of good food again. How simple our ambitions then!

Stickman

A/T Snodgrass had a plan, that with bulled boots he'd be stickman
When mounting guard, he'd show the rest how smart he was, and with well pressed
Trousers he'd be sure to score, while others stagged, he could snore
At leisure in his comfy bed - let others stand on guard instead.

So, with his new boots in his hand, and red hot handled spoon as planned,
He laboured long into the night, burned and polished, till first light
Saw Snoddys boots, a work of art, a sight to lift a Sergeants heart.
The glossy sheen like ebony shone, and in his heart, he knew he'd won.

When time came for the guard to mount, our Snoddy tried, on no account
To let his shiny boots be marred by accidental kicks, and hard
As others really tried, as stickman then, he would preside.
For this was his big moment, when, his labours wouldn't be in vain.

" Guard, Shun !" The order rang out loud, and Snoddy, keen, and oh, so proud,
Picked up his left foot, slammed it down, but as the sole bit in the ground,
The toecap, gleaming, flew away, and much to Snoddys great

dismay,
Exposed a big toe, shining bright, through rotten sock. Oh, what a sight !

So Snoddys plan all came to nought, but could have worked, if he had thought
When, spoon in hand, he'd made a point of missing stitches at the joint
Where toecap meets the upper part, he wouldn't finish in the cart.
All of which just shows, I guess, that graft don't always mean success !

TeeCee

Thanks for the memories

Thanks for the memories….
Of freezing cold parades
With all our new young mates,
Or in our best SD there,
Stood at 80 in the shade,
How sweaty it was.

Thanks for the memories….
Of greasy burnt stale toast,
And what we hated most,
Dehydrated spud,
Or cold bread pud,
Or things undiagnosed,
How hungry we were.

We were all just innocent, green boys then,
Unknowing, unsuspecting naïve children,
But we soon got the message loud and clear when
We were rudely awoke by a loud, uncouth bloke…..

Thanks for the memories…..
Of learning to get on
With lads we'd normally shun
And thinking more of others
Instead of Number One,
And mucking in with joke and grin
Till rotten jobs were done,
We learned, soon, so much.

Thanks for the memories…..
Of breaking out of school,

And thinking it was cool,
Then getting caught and being taught
That breaking all the rules
Was not allowed and we just showed
That we were silly fools,
How stupid we were!

We lived life in a constant, giddy whirl when
We thought that we were Gods own gift to girls then,
But then we were deluded, dreaming, young men,
So, "What the Hell!", then, we'd say, let's live for the day!

Thanks for the memories.....
For now we're getting on,
Let's face it, it was fun,
Not at the time, but never mind
The recollections come
Tumbling from the memory
And when all is said and done,
How lucky we were.

Thanks for the memories.....
Of bashing lumps of steel
With enthusiastic zeal,
Producing squares and hexagons,
And blisters, all too real,
How painful it was!

Thanks for the memories.....
Of going down the town,
Then wandering around
And beating up the local lads
Who tried to do us down,
How bloody it was!

We lived on a few shillings easily then,
'Cos Blanco and Brasso were really cheap then,
We thought that we were rich going on leave when
The credits we saved were finally paid….

Thanks for the memories…..
Of Uncle Fred's hotel
We got to know so well,
On jankers and on fire crew,
Listening to his dulcet yell,
How funny he was.

Thanks for the memories…..
Of walking through that gate,
And wondering what our fate
Would be, when after three
Years we would finally be free,
How anxious we were!

Thanks for the memories….
Of Sundays that were free,
No early Reveille,
Lie in your pit, then in a bit,
Your breakfast – leisurely!
How civilised it was.

TeeCee

A.A.S. Memorial 2014

Although some places that they knew are now no longer there,
This corner of our native soil will still be here to bear
Witness to the youth of this fair land of ours, when they
Pledged loyally to serve Nation and Monarch, come what may.

Instructed in their tradesman's skills with expertise well learned
While growing up in comradeship, they formed a bond that burned
Long in their hearts when they departed on their chosen way,
But always to remember those early, youthful days.

For Sixty years and more these boys came to their country's aid
In peace and war around the world; the difference that they made
Helped to ensure our military earned world-wide admiration,
By working tirelessly with grit and quiet determination.

For those whose cost of this commitment was to prove so high,
This quiet place is their true home, no matter where they lie;
Remembering what they began with youthful expectation,
But ending much too soon in pursuit of this land's salvation.

So sit upon these seats before you, read all that you see,
For this is an important part of our own history,
Maybe not the stories of the heroes, brave and bold,
But in it's own momentous way, a tale that should be told.

And now, as we stand here, united in our common cause,
Our thoughts perhaps of days long gone, the time has come to pause,
Remembering how we all came to be the very part
Of this, our proud fraternity, dear to all our hearts.

Ensuring that our story will remain, though years may fade
The memory of our being, and the difference that we made
Through many years of faithful service in the Army's ranks,
Earning well deserved acclaim, and a grateful Nation's thanks.

TeeCee

Goodbye Arborfield

There's a little place in Berkshire County, down by Reading way,
It isn't very big, quite undistinguished, some might say.
And yet, it's known by thousands, maybe millions, mostly men
Who came and spent some time there, passing through or, then again,
Returning to it regularly over many years,
A place for some of memorable times, for others new careers.

It all began there well over one hundred years ago,
The army needed horses, hence a large remount depot
Was located at the village, being accommodation for
The horses which passed through on their way to the First Great War;
And when the war was ended, it then was left unused
For horses were redundant, as the war had clearly proved.

But then, as years elapsed and war clouds gathered yet once more,
This place became the birthplace of a fledgling military Corps
Forged from the fiery furnace of war's technical demands,
From fields of Europe to the distant, far-off desert sands,
It gathered all the artisans from home and overseas
Who came together, founding a great Army dynasty.

So, from this first beginning in those troubled, war-torn years,
The Corps of Royal Electrical and Mechanical Engineers
Carved out a name, so well deserved, for skill and expertise,

In their demanding role in seeing that the Army's wheels
Kept turning at those crucial times of triumph or disaster,
When first class training would decide who was the final master.

And this is where this place, this village with its leafy lanes
Has welcomed thousands of young men and boys to come and train
In technical achievement to maintain, repair, inspect
All manner of devices due to damage or neglect,
Some were volunteers who came to make a fine career,
While others served their National Service after training here.

But in these modern times, when change is often made by those
Who sit in judgement far away in remote, lofty pose,
Complacency is ill advised, and facts somehow contrive,
To change, and in collective wisdom, the time has now arrived
For all that once had gone before, that place of work and play
Is now gone while a new chapter is opened far away.

And what of Arborfield where all those memories reside?
A history distinguished, now fated to be filed
In musty books, a passing phase – hardly worth a glance
To those who in the future come to read it just by chance.
But to us who still remember it with reminiscent smile
It stands as proud as any place in this, our Sceptre'd Isle!

TeeCee

Arborfield Revisited

Quiet now, its time is done, no more the young men, all long gone;
The road, which passed these lonely gates, is just a lane that now awaits
It's fate, now daily drawing near, erasing all that we held dear,
Consigning all that used to be to the odd page of history.

But how can the lone printed word describe the things that had occurred
Within those boundaries we'd known? The lives that changed; things that were done?
And dedicated people who had helped to mould us, seen us through
Those early years as we grew strong, teaching us the right from wrong?

The trees, still here, are taller now, though all else seems much smaller now
Than we recall from memory; the spaces where there used to be
Long lines of wooden huts, alive with sounds of youthful noise, survive
Now only in the recollection of those years, with fond affection.

The eerie sense of dissipation underlines the isolation
Of the place where we once stood, of days that we lived, bad and good,
The same place that we left back then, vowing never to again
Return or see, once we had gone - so foolish, looking back,

years on.

This place of so much history has seen times, which will ever be
Remembered by those who took part in bygone years; events which start
To strike a chord and in surprise, a certain moistness of the eyes
Is felt; quite why, we cannot tell, emotion that's hard to dispel.

The gentle rustling of the breeze and birdsong in the myriad trees
Are now the only, lonely sounds disturbing this peace all around,
Where once the tramp of boots was heard, and carried on the wind, the words
Of barked command, both loud and clear, the very essence of life here.

Echoes, echoes of the past, images remain and last
Forever in our late recall, people that we knew and all
Liked and respected - some we feared - others, popular, we cheered.
Enjoying friendly company with happy equanimity.

We'll say our final, fond farewell and hope that those who come to dwell
Upon this land that we called home will have in a remembrance, some
Small token of our great affection for this place, no real objection
Could be surely raised by those who in their turn will follow us?

Tech School, Boys School, take your pick, we're proud of it, so let it stick
In the collective memory of those who will in future be
Custodians of this honoured place, and not allow time to erase
Those past glories that should survive, to keep that famed renown alive.

TeeCee

Boys No More

The great adventure had begun,
We'd left our families, homes and gone
Away into the great unknown,
Apprehensive, feeling lost, alone,
And wondering what the future held,
Our hopes, though high, fear undispelled.

Then suddenly, no time to think,
Life's one long round of work, eat, drink,
Sleep. Spit and polish rule our lives,
Yet slowly, imperceptibly arrives
The bonds of friendship, long to last
Throughout the years, strong and steadfast.

Friendships forged by joy and pain,
Shared escapades of loss and gain,
Yes, truly we were brothers all,
Stronger ties than blood recall
The mutual feelings that we shared,
And how we laughed and joked and cared.

We see them still through memory's haze,
The bright, long, glorious, carefree days,
When youth enjoyed the summer long,
Erased, the hard times, strife and gone
The times when we felt low,
Just golden days in mind's eye grow.

But time exacts its bitter toll,
And young men age, grow frail and fall
Prey to the ever rolling years,

Life's toil and pain, sadness, tears,
No more the boys of days long past,
Till finally life ebbs, at last.

Yet though life's span has run its course,
No need for anger, fear, remorse,
But privileged to have shared in part
The life of those, who from the start
Had given friendship unreserved,
No better epitaph deserved!

So we were blessed, much more than most,
To have that comradeship, though lost
In passing years our youth,
Those ties still bind and yet, in truth
They live on, young, as when first we met,
They don't grow old.

We won't forget.

TeeCee

Fifty Names

Fifty names marked time's inexorable march down through the years
In that cool wooded corner, as we listened there were tears
Of sad remembrance as they were called out there, one by one,
While we recalled those times when we were all so very young.

The dappled shade amid this circle of surrounding trees
Helped cool the sun's fierce glare, and with a passing, gentle breeze,
We stood, as bugle's call, so poignant, sounded the 'Last Post',
And Pipes, a sad lament, then faded from the listening host.

And yet, a sense of some completeness came that they'd returned
To be applauded by their friends, those that they loved, and earned

This final accolade of a good life, lived fair and true,
According to those values we had learned as years ensued.

So as our voices lifted through those trees in songs of praise,
It may be that they heard and smiled in their celestial space,
And joined in spirit with all those of us who still remain,
Until that time when we will be reunited once again.

TeeCee

Final Chapter (Saying farewell to the founding intakes)

And so our final chapter is drawing to a close,
Times wheel, it turns inexorably, taking with it those
We thought as indestructible, but physically so,
For spiritually they'll always be as real as long ago:
Though maybe not of our own time, it is well understood
That we are all related in exclusive brotherhood
Of common, warm endeavour, of faithful, loyal heart,
Each one of us is surely still a strong integral part
Of that which time will not deny, nor ever fail to be
Less than a sure commitment to our camaraderie.

And as we bid farewell to those we held in high esteem,
We recognise how fortunate we all were to have been
Privileged to be part of the same fraternity
Of which they were a founding member, and will always be
Honoured and remembered as a good and gentle men,
A great reminder of how fine a person really can
Become, by living to the truths they learned as a young boy,
And practising throughout a life of hard work to enjoy
The fruits of happiness, devoted family at their side,
Who loved and cherished him, with quiet dignity and pride.

So sleep your sleep old warriors, it's surely well deserved,
Your time in this world never wasted, loyally you served
Country, King, and fellow man the best that you knew how,
And after a successful life, it's time, at long last, now,
To say farewell and we know, at those other welcome gates,
Your old friends who have gone before, are gathering to await
Their old brother in arms, laughing, as they did when they
First met as long ago in early happy, youthful days.
And "The Reds" will echo out, that half forgotten serenade,

As another Old Boy makes his final Passing Out Parade.

TeeCee

Final Curtain

And so at last the curtain falls, the lights dim on a stage, now bare;
The players all dispersed and gone, returning whence they journeyed there.
And all around, the silence, now so deafening in its solitude,
Lies like a mantle, or a shroud, mourning for the multitude
Of lithe young men who graced this part of leafy England down the years,
Who now with sadness view this place, as time demands its tariff, dear.

Now gone, the bustling, busy sounds that shattered early morning peace,
Imperious bugle calls to signal new days dawn, and on the breeze
Aromas from the cookhouse door, provoking nostrils, sweet torment
For youths, who, permanently starving, pledged stomach's replenishment.
And through it all, a sense of urgency, insistent pressing need,
So much to do, so little time, 'twas ever the apprentice creed.

So farewell, site of former glories, memory's repository,
We who traversed through your era will forever grateful be
For the spirit you engendered, for the brotherhood you gave,
And the time we saw together, looking to a future, brave.
Your future will not be momentous – that, you have already been,
You will now revert to be a part of this domestic scene.

But to us who lived with you at different times through years of change,
You will always be remembered as that place we entered, strange
At first, but viewed quite fondly through the mists of times long gone
As the starting point in adult life that we had then embarked upon.

Arborfield, you served your country, just as surely as all those
Who passed between those gates, which finally now, at last, regretfully close;
No room for emotional farewells, progress must be satisfied,
(But for now, some may not feel that they would still remain dry eyed…..)

TeeCee

Old Comrades

If you're ill and feeling low,
Cheer up, because you'll always know
Your pals from way back will be there
To share the pain, or maybe bear,
Or help to bear life's onward toll,
And give support to those who fall
From fitness peak, to depths unsung,
With lessons learned when we were young,
To help our friends to carry on,
Till all adversity is gone.
So hang on in there, force a grin,
You never were trained to give in
To setbacks great, or troubles small,
Your chums will rally, give their all
To help you back till you have won,
Stay with it lad – you're not alone !

TeeCee

Friendship

It can't be seen, it has no form nor still cannot be heard,
And to some, it means no more than any other word.
But yet it has a power so strong that if it could be sold,
No earthly price would e'er suffice, no untold weight of gold.

We, who at a tender age left home and flew the nest
Were fortunate, for we soon found this thing before the rest
Became aware of how it can affect us, heart and soul,
Forever at its mercy, it's perpetual control.

At first we didn't notice as it crept into our lives
As we adjusted in our new world merely to survive,
It's surreptitious presence, very quietly begun,
Meant we were all affected, and submitted, one by one.

It is now only at this stage of life that we can see
What power there is in something that we feel so readily,
That old, familiar feeling that comes flooding back again,
To wrap us in that glow of comfort, so hard to explain.

The freedom, so instinctive, that makes us carry on
With conversations started then, though fifty years have gone.
The feeling all of two score years was just an interlude,
A moments pause to draw a breath while savouring the mood.

It's a pair of old worn slippers that we wear inside our head,
Friendly, comforting and snug, with thoughts and words unsaid,
To make us feel at home again, among our youthful peers,

Recalling all the fun we had, while rolling back the years.

Of course, it's Friendship that we share; to some, a passing phase,
But not I think, for most of us, who lived those long gone days,
We shared a common lifestyle then, through times of joy and woe,
And now enjoy that friendship which began so long ago.

It doesn't matter when we served, or how much time has flown,
The comradeship that was born then, still spans the years long gone,
And our exclusive Brotherhood, have learned what time has taught,
That we will always share that thing that never can be bought.

.... True Friendship

TeeCee

Happy New Year

We've come a long way since that very first day
When we stepped gingerly through those gates,
Since then we have seen many changes,
And been to strange places and made lots of mates.
While through the long years that have passed,
We have tried to adhere to those friends from the past,
But the passage of time and diversions meanwhile
Meant we strayed much too far, much too fast,
And in consequence we can almost lose sense
Of that special attachment we had,
So to lose the recall of the times we all shared,
Would be surely too tragically sad.

But now that the Web is here, we have the chance to cheer
And re-establish once more,
The friendships we treasured along with the pleasure
That we had in our memory's store.
So as we discover and start to recover
Those mates that we thought had long gone,
And meet once again, swing the lamp,
While obtaining the updates of what had been done,
We now can give greetings to all at this meeting place,
Even to those far away,
A Happy New Year to you all, and those dear to you,
May laughter fill each every day.

TeeCee

Last Parade

Silenced now, this hallowed ground,
No more to echo and resound
To barked commands, the beating drum,
The bugle, calling all to come
To muster, or to beat retreat,
In winters chill and summers heat.

The ghosts are still there, looking down,
And Sergeant Majors grimace, frown,
That it has come to this, their dream,
The place where they once ruled supreme,
Is now a desolate, lost space,
Their pride, now tainted, in disgrace.

Forlorn, untended now, it lies,
With cracks and weeds in slow demise.
Flanked by two pillars, mute and gaunt,
Once welcoming, but now to haunt
The memory of what had been,
Guardians of the changing scene.

Greensward now rings this lonely square,
Where wooden buildings once stood there,
And echoes of youths, in their prime,
Resound down corridors of time,
Bringing poignant memories,
Of former glories, in reprise.

The garden occupies the space
Where Guardroom once took pride of place,
Now, standing testament of where

Young boys began to learn, prepare
For life, in military role,
Succumbs, as progress takes its toll.

But, while there still exists a man,
Who proudly can proclaim, " I am
An ex-boy out of Arborfield",
Then this old square will never yield,
Or ever be forgot by they
Who knew it in its glory day.

TeeCee

Our Legacy

History tells us that nought will endure,
And time vanquishes all, which - though seeming secure
In our hearts and our minds - are but transient things
That arrive and depart on Eternity's wings.
So it is our duty for those yet to come,
To record for posterity all that was done
And achieved by those thousands of young boys who all
Came to willingly serve, answering duty's call.

We leave a clear message to those who will come
To this quiet corner, and also to some
Of the families who will garner comfort and pride
From the stonemasons art where the name blocks provide
The actual structure, joined closely, as one,
Rather as in those first years, these boys' lives had done,
When they bonded in friendship and learned how to share
The good and the bad times with all whom were there.

So tread these steps gently, read names etched in stone,
Each one has a tale to tell, and of things done
Which deserve this remembrance of duty and trust
For the services rendered; for each name there must
Be thousands of others, not named, in the thoughts
Of their comrades who lived their young lives and were taught
The real values of life as they grew into men,
In these places of learning where they first began.

Those places are now very sadly all gone,
But the work and the ethos born there still lives on
In the hearts and the minds of all those who survive

With that brotherhood which we all shared, still alive.
Therefore let this occasion be full of good cheer,
We should celebrate now with all who attend here
And thank our committee whose hard work and vision
Have brought this project to successful fruition.
TeeCee

Musical Memories

What can stir a thought that's buried deep within the soul?
Some say that it could be the sense of smell,
But I prefer to think perhaps, the power of recall
Is wakened when melodic rhythms swell
And spill into the memory of days so long ago,
When voices young and lusty start to sing
Together for the hell of it, the words we used to know,
And really made the old roof rafters' ring.

It could have been a hymn or something from the hit parade,
Or some song parodied, as squaddies do,
Where it may have come from, or whatever sound it made,
The meaning would be changed to something blue!
Yet music in all shapes and forms can have the same effect
Of dredging from the mind those recollections,
The 'British Grenadiers' will likely readily connect
To eight bars, (fifteen paces), on reflection.

Similarly 'Scipio', or then, 'Scotland the Brave'
May suddenly transport the unsuspecting
Listener back in time to when these tunes were so engraved
On the memory banks, sharp, suddenly connecting.
"It hath the power to soothe the savage breast," the poet wrote,
And there's no doubt it leaves a marked impression
On subconscious minds, just lying there, forgotten and remote,
Till distant sounds rekindle resurrection.

What else is there that so inspires, and yet can move to tears,

When folk hear old familiar music played,
Bringing back to consciousness while rolling back the years,
Recalling life in song and serenade?
And we, whose lives were ordered and dictated by the sound
Of the bugle, with those calls so loud and clear,
Have more cause to remember these things, permanently bound
To those ringing notes across the Barrack Square.

A piece of music can point to a milestone in a life,
Touching every single one who hears
Or yet again, provide a bond that husband and a wife
Share, theirs to prize and cherish through the years;
But most of all its value is within its power to calm,
To pacify and soothe the troubled mind,
Comforting and helping rid those feelings of alarm,
If harnessed, what a gift to all mankind!

TeeCee

Old Boys - Old Soldiers

Their hair is greyer, growing thin, the eyes less keen, waists less trim,
Yet in their hearts they're still sixteen, young now, as they'd ever been.
Though time creeps on, on silent feet, the memories, so bittersweet,
Come flooding back to fond recall, when once again they meet, and all
The years evaporate, they're in their prime once more with mates
Whose nicknames, given, when so young, appear as though they'd never gone.

The easy comfort that they feel when with old friends, returns to seal
Them in a personal, private state, which no one could appreciate,
Unless, like them, they'd shared their life - the good, the bad, the joy, the strife.
They slip back into ways of speech. Words, long forgotten oft-time, reach
Into the brain's subconsciousness, igniting memories in the quest
To bring to mind events long gone, when days were sunny, summers long.

The camaraderie warms the heart, captures time when at the start
Of their careers, when fresh and young, all to gain, on the first rung
Of life's long ladder, climbing up, try to achieve to gain the

top
Of their profession, strong and bold, success was there, to have and hold.
But older now and wiser too, they reminisce and think of who
Had started with them, now long gone, and count those left to carry on.

The lessons learned so long ago, which shaped their lives and helped them grow
Into the men they are today, have helped them travel life's highway
And meet the challenges it brings, to overcome the many things
That might bring lesser persons down, unfortunate that they'd not grown
In youthful company of their peers, during those important years
Of laughs and jokes, eventful days, influenced in so many ways.

At first it seems at casual glance that it's old sweats recalling once
Again their soldiering days gone by, yet there is more than meets the eye
To this. They think of times now gone, when promises, relied upon
Would be kept, the consciousness of folk in general still was less
Directed to material things, truth and honour which then brings
Our lives into a higher plane - virtues we won't see again.

The hectic pace of life lived now, the onward rush to gain somehow

At cost of conscience, wealth and fame, no motive now to 'play the game',
Just blunder on, ignore the rest, the selfishness, will now attest
That values Old Boys learned are dead, and greed, self interest, rule instead.
That's why they prize these moments, when they turn back time to live again
In the gentler, honest age they knew, among those friends so good and true.

TeeCee

One Old Boy's Reunion

I recognised him straight away, the passing years had been quite kind,
That old, familiar, friendly grin, the honest face, the agile mind.
As if the three score years since we last saw each other, slipped away,
We talked of things that we had done as if 't'was only yesterday,
The recollections of our pals, the scrapes and bruises that we shared,
And latterly, the diverse paths we'd taken, how our lives had fared.

Enveloped in our private world, our own personal comfort zone,
We chatted as the time flew by, of past events, the things we'd done.
But time's a hard taskmaster too, and all too soon we had to be
Returning via different roads, reverted to the reality
Of modern times, the alien world so far removed from those we knew,
When we were young and full of life with optimistic point of view.

But then that was a year ago, and though I looked and searched in vain,
No sign of him at this reunion, till I chanced to hear his name
Read out on this year's roll of honour. Stunned, I hardly could believe

He, once so full of life could now be gone, yet sadly to concede
That we who have led such full lives must know this is just a way
Of telling us that still remain, to live and value every day.

So, after the initial sadness, thinking of what might have been,
What other escapades recalled, what future fun we might have seen,
I think that when my own time comes, and my tomorrow fails to dawn,
I will look forward to that time when life's curtains are finally drawn,
And we will meet again, somewhere, resume what we'd begun,
Continue that old friendship at that last reunion.

TeeCee

Our Glorious Past

Just a bare, sparse patch of ground.
A car park? Yes – but what's that sound?
The skirl of pipes, a bugle call,
The tramp of feet, shouts mingle,
All around the ghosts are here,
Most, young, fresh faced, eyes eager, clear,
And others, older, stern of face,
All uniformed and with a grace
Of movement, a daily learned routine,
With heads held high, a polished sheen
Reflecting in the morning sun,
The glorious past parades again.

A ghostly roll-call echoes on,
Names well remembered, one by one,
MacNally, Cook, Brady, Cole,
Sallis, Silver and Huxley, all
Of those recalled from yesteryear
Who earned respect (and sometimes fear!)
The memories, undimmed by time
Of tears and comradeship sublime,
Return again when we recalled
How things once were, when we stood tall,
Prepared to face the future, proud,
To take on the world with heads unbowed.

So just a patch of ground? Maybe.
But it masks a long proud history
Of values gained, the will to strive,
Directions taken, the zest to live.
So if upon that ground you go

And hear a ghostly bugle blow,
Remember all that once was there,
And in remembrance, say a prayer

TeeCee

Remembering

Frosty winter mornings, steaming breath hangs in the air,
Wishing we were somewhere else, away from sergeants glare.
Crunching gravel underfoot, rhythmic, tedious tread,
Marching round, when we would sooner be back in our bed!
This daily ritual was the one that we tried to evade,
But mostly there was no escape from the Muster Parade,
The stamping boots, the barked commands a noisy, loud affair
Marching round in circles, never going anywhere.

Not so bad in summertime, we were at least quite warm,
And shirtsleeve order generally made it easy to perform
The wheeling, slow and quick time marching movements that we made,

(And we thought that we'd all joined up to simply learn a trade!)
But still, it kept us really fit, quite healthy and suntanned,
While some of the more crafty lads joined one of the school bands.
Then, in the warmth and comfort of the band room they could stay
Out of the bawling, nasty 'orrible Sergeant Major's way.

Then hunger. Gnawing all-pervading feeling of starvation,
The griping pangs that clutched our guts, that aching, drained sensation
Of never ending emptiness endured with fortitude,
Along with sex, our waking thoughts were mainly lewd, and food!
We nicked the bread and spirited the marmalade and butter
Away at breakfast time, so in the evening we could cut a
Loaf up into nice thick bits and, failing fires to fry on,
We made the toast by using our room's sole electric iron.

It worked a treat, so we enjoyed our toast - all nice and hot,
But when time came to press our best kit, if we had forgot
To clean the flat plate of the iron immediately we'd used it,
The blackened crummy face showed how we'd callously abused it,
And much hard scraping, scouring, buffing, following a soak
Was needed – still, it did give us experience in doing a decoke!
But then, what we <u>did</u> learn were all the ways to improvise,
Which came in useful later in some dubious schemes devised.

These may be the events that faded into distant past,
Yet at the time their impact on our life was truly vast,
But it engendered virtues, although we were unaware,

The instinct to succeed despite all setbacks started there,
Along with self reliance, coupled with the comradeship
That held us much more firmly than we knew, in timely grip.
So all in all, we did OK, pursuing lives diverse,
We made the right choice, and, you know, we could have done much worse!

TeeCee

Reunion 2012 a New Experience

We travelled in from far and near, but not to Arborfield I fear,
For progress had at last decreed that housing for the folks in need
Must take priority, and so the Alma Mater had to go.
But though we're sad at its demise, we long ago learned to improvise
So with no further time to waste, new ground was sought to celebrate
Our annual reunion bash, and get best value for our cash.

We found a place in Leicestershire, a venue big enough for hire
To cater for our merry crew of displaced persons seeking new
Agreeable cheap, nice locations for our annual celebration.

I think we mostly would agree that this hotel turned out to be
More than equal to the task, coping with not just us, but vast
Incoming hordes from who knows where, to various weddings performed there.

Some would say not 'cheap' but then, we'll ne'er pay mess prices again,
Those days are gone, we'll grin and bear it, tolerate the pain and share it,
Like we did in days gone by, but just for now we can but try
To look upon those golden days when at reunions we could stay
In those old spiders that we knew, turn back the clock for just a few
Hours, living our young lives again, savouring what we knew then.

But now the present must be faced, to make the best of this new place,
For why? It could turn out to be where we'll again meet regularly.
The location is central for the whole country, whereas before,
The Jocks and Geordies had to drive, arriving more dead than alive,
But soon revived miraculously when they had had a pint or three
Forced down their throats, despite protests (although not many, one suspects!)

We journeyed on the following day to Alweras, not far away;
A coach ride of an hour, just less, where we, accompanied by our guests

Gathered round the circled dais, our newly dedicated place,
That fine Memorial where we stood, and waiting in that quiet wood
To hold, as in days of yore, our Drumhead Service as before.
Surroundings changed, but hymns and prayers familiar to our waiting ears.

Yet as we sang and said those prayers, the feeling then of being there
To call to mind our friends now gone, it seemed, with these names marked in stone,
That there could be no better place to pause, reflect upon those days
When we, so young with futures bright, saw all in optimistic light;
And as the haunting Last Post played, notes shimmering through that leafy glade,
It seemed that in this setting, we had found the perfect place to be.

Then, back to base for AGM, and dress for dinner, here again
All went quite well, and our tradition continued on with the rendition
Of the Pipers call to eat as all filed in to take their seats
For a meal enjoyed by all, then, after speeches, came the call
To give voice to our Battle Hymn, that song that we were proud to sing,
"The Reds"!, Sang with all zest and flair, to end a memorable evening there

This year, with all the changes seen has not by any measure been
An easy one it has been said, yet still we seem to keep ahead

And make progress through thick and thin, but this, we know, is due again
To our committee and their work on our behalf, they do not shirk
In finding us that which we need, so let us recognise their deeds
Of selfless service, every one, and give a great heartfelt WELL DONE!!

TeeCee

Reunion Ode

They journeyed back from far and near, to swing the lamp again,
Wearing out their hobnailed boots, as they marched down memory lane.
The Old Boys gather once a year to celebrate their past,
They drink a toast, good health, and cheer their friendships holding fast.
They march, heads high, the medals glint, and year's just fall away,
As once again they stand in line, as true as yesterday.

Then, in silence, gathered round the solitary gates,
The garden by the hallowed ground, where the ghost of Fred still waits,
Remembering comrades, the times they shared, who's final posting came,
And now stand watch on heavenly guard, to muster once again.
Onward then, to celebrate the golden boys now here,
The toasts and speeches dedicate their fifty glorious years.
And afterwards, well fed, content, the same old questions rise,
"Who was that guy? Know where he went ? The laughs, the jokes – the sighs.

And so, they all prepare once more, to go their separate ways,
Old bonds renewed, strong to endure, goodwill that never strays.
The buildings now are long, long gone, a history mark in time,
But the spirit of the boys lives on, in men now in their prime.

They keep it fresh, each year renew that special feeling when,
In twelve months time they'll all return, to do it once again
….. And again… and again!

TeeCee

The Reds

"Cheers, Cheers The REDS are HERE
What the hell to we care?
What the hell to we care?
Cheers, Cheers The Reds are Here
What the hell do we care now?
For it's a Grand old School to fight for,
For it's a Grand old Song to sing.
When you hear its history,
It's enough to make your heart feel G...L...A ...D !!!!
We don't care what (Carlisle, Harrogate, Chepstow *) say,
As on our way we go,
For we only know that there's gonna' be a show
And the RED supporters will be there
They're at the NAAFI,
Queuing up for buckshie tea,
Without the sugar
Queuing up for buckshie tea,"
* Depending upon where you were at the time of singing...

Sir Arthur Sullivan composed the tune and Gilbert the vocal score,
But the Arborfield lads didn't much like the words, so decided to invent a few more.
And that was the birth of the school battle hymn, (although no-one knows, really, quite when,)
Which was captured by myriad thousand young voices, time and time over again.

It rang across the footballing fields and resounded around the camp hall,
And visiting teams came to fear, soon, the sound, as a

harbinger of their downfall.
Many a boxer hanging over the ropes really thought that his last hour had come,
Till, faint, far away, through the mist of the pain came the strains of that inspiring song.

Like a shot of adrenaline via his heart, it exploded straight into his brain,
Then, revitalized, he bent to his task to the ever-repeated refrain.
With the sound in his ears of exuberant cheers, he pounded and punched with aplomb,
Till the poor adversary, who had thought he was winning, soon found out that something was wrong.

For he then realized that he wasn't just facing one person alone in the ring,
And, at first undaunted, he found himself haunted by THE tune they started to sing.
So, love it or not, "The Reds" holds a slot in most Old Boys long standing affection,
For it marked at that time the team spirit sublime that's remembered in fond recollection.

But as years rolled along, the strains of the song faded into the past, now long gone,
And the voices, so youthful which sang it so tuneful, are now just a low baritone.
'Cos the lads who remembered it now are quite aged, and feeling a tiny bit sad,
For that song represented our youth and recalled the great unity, once, that we had.

Sixty Up!

No parking meters, yellow lines along the roads, no instant fines
To catch the driver so unwary, saluting AA men, the very
Essence of the way we were, fresh from the war and breathing air
Of a free country, dearly bought by countrymen who stood and fought
To gain this precious gift, ensuring freedom for us all, enduring.

Milkmen whistling in the dawn, clanking bottles, hooves clomp on
The quiet gas-lit cobbled streets as the old horse patrols his beat
And, pulling on the laden cart he labours on, a very part
Of life in early Fifties then, picking up the threads of peace again.
Returning once more to the days of normal life, domestic ways.

Then, on one February day, our King just quietly passed away,
Worn out leading his tired nation, overseeing our salvation,
Gaining grateful thanks deserved from those whom he most loyally served,
And passing on the monarchs role to a young girl to be the sole
Ruler in his recent stead, a heavy crown for her young head.

And at this time it so contrived that in this month there then arrived

A motley bunch of callow youths, all no doubt searching for the truth
In that old adage "Be a soldier", and, before they were much older
Saw the error of their ways, looking at the long dark days
That stretched ahead for three long years, yes, some must have shed bitter tears.

But no! It didn't look so bad once they'd got used to it, and had
A few months of the give and take of army life, and learned to make
The best of what they'd signed on for, and knew then, just what lay in store
For those in intake Fifty-Two A, their fate was then, from that first day
Effectively, for all time sealed, inside the gates of Arborfield.

Now, three-score years have come and gone, and that young lady soldiers on,
But then, no less, have those young lads, though now their role is of Granddads,
Who, like her Majesty, has seen it come to pass and mostly been
There, done it all, got the tee shirt, have shared the glory and the dirt
That comes to soldiers now and then, but willingly do it all again.

So raise your glasses all you jeeps, and senior divs to she who keeps
The name of Queen with dignity, and also to those lads who she
Shares with, this diamond celebration, a cause for cheer and jubilation
To be heard throughout this land. And for us lads, a rousing hand
Of loud applause to mark the day those lads were christened, Fifty-Two A !!

Soya Sausages

Flat and square, that's what they were, and came wrapped up in tin,
No skins to peel, 'cos they weren't real, and relatively thin.
Invented when real meat was scarce, but nourishing and good,
The troops consumed them by the ton, a well-liked type of food.

The things that they would do with them sometimes surpassed belief,
They'd hang the tins in engine bays, or sometimes underneath
A hot exhaust, which warmed them up, while trundling on their way,
Ready for the next brew up, or dinner for the day.

But it was most important, if this method was employed,
To pierce the tin before its contents came to be enjoyed.
For failure to observe this rule could lead to mass destruction
When Soya'd decorate the works, upon the loud eruption!

But now, alas, they are quite scarce, as tastes are changing now,
No more, the succulent repast that taste buds came to know.
They've gone into the mists of time, old soldiers all regret
There's nothing in this modern age, remotely like them - yet!

Spirit

I am the flickering shadow that haunts the Old School Square,
The lingering, echoing, bugle calls that fill the evening air,
I am the ghost of thousands smartly marching in the dawn,
The tramping, rhythmic sounds disturbing early, misty morn.

I am the memory of the countless, carefree, happy days,
The laughter and the fun that came so many different ways,
I am the sadness when that life too soon came to an end,
The knowledge, later on in life, there were no better friends.

I am the guardian of those who were there to guide and teach,
The patience and composure as young minds they tried to reach.
I am the recollection of upstanding military men,
The fine example of what real soldiers were, was there in them.

I am these things which will, in this place now, for all time be,
Though signs of that existence will fade from the memory,
The spirit of those who found a new life here will never die,
And in the fabric of this place, forever will reside.

Future generations living in this special place
May think they sometimes hear a sound, although they cannot trace
The source of this disturbance, it will very likely be
A ghostly bugle playing the "Lights Out" or "Reveille."

And I, the spirit of all these will haunt the leafy lanes,

Remembering forever as the sounds are heard again
Of regimental music floating on the evening breeze,
Gently fading into silence, 'midst the rustling of the leaves.

A thousand lusty, youthful voices joining in as one,
And once again "The Reds" will resonate as it had done
In bygone years, and men now grey with age will nod and smile,
And live again those happy years, for just a little while.

TeeCee

The Gates of Fate

They stand, no more to welcome youth, in wretched isolation,
Yet, if they had the power of speech they'd speak of the occasions
Of what they'd seen in countless years of youngsters passing through
Their arch, proclaiming to those boys, a life starting anew.

A life of learning to succeed in chosen skilled vocations
Acquiring wisdom as they learned, with wit and toleration;
Toleration, discipline, that transforms men from boys
Who go into the adult world with confidence and poise.

Those gates which welcomed all into exclusive brotherhood

Would tell tales of events that changed the world for bad or good,
Of grief and sadness, joy and laughter, through the years gone by,
Yet keeping the remembrance of a spirit time defies.

We'd hear of Commandants departures, towed by cheering lads,
Of Sergeant Majors of all kinds, the good ones and the bad.
Their barked commands for all to hear, across the old school square
The sound of bugles, pipes and drums, hanging in the air.

They'd mention how they opened to admit the parents so
They'd see how sons had fared from leaving home and how they'd grown
Into those robust, healthy soldiers, disciplined and smart,
Making fathers proud and stealing all the female hearts.

Yet they were of their time, and must succumb to time's progression,
And soon they'll be no more in that inexorable succession,
But in the minds of those who passed between those gates so young
They'll be there, indestructible, till all that knew are gone.

TeeCee

The Ghosts

The leafy lanes of Berkshire will not be quite the same,
Those martial sounds – once, all around – will not be heard again,
Familiar beating drums and fleeting thoughts of what had been,
Will fade and fall into recall for some that shared that dream.

A Dream? Yes, it will seem so in the years that are to be,
A ghostly dream so far removed from the reality
Of rows of houses, shops, and all those common, mundane things,
In everyday existence that normality always brings.

And only in the minds of those who occupied this place,
Will this dream be reality from past times, though a trace
Of some remembrance should exist to mark that which had been
So meaningful to this locality in years between.

A school of thought exists that in the fabric of a place,
There is a latent memory that can never be erased
Of all that happened in the years now gone from long-ago,
Ghosts of the past who haunt the leafy lanes we used to know.

The echo of a thousand bugle calls ring down the ages,
Sounds of hoof-beats pounding through countless history's pages,
Young men arriving from the farthest corners of the earth,

Serving, learning how to fight for things, they thought, of worth.

And boys, in the first flush of youth, starting down life's road,
Embarking on life changing paths, secure in the accord
Bestowed by wise and learned men, skilled in the many arts
Of burgeoning technology, to help them play their part.

This place of knowledge, discipline, of skill and dedication
Has served this Nation constantly, and helped in it's salvation
From threats, providing fighting men, skilled artisans that fought,
Some dying for the freedom, so clearly, dearly bought.

And maybe, in the coming years, when all who knew are gone,
The ones who occupy this place may hear a distant song,
Or maybe, on a summer's evening walk, may stop and pause,
And hear the sound of martial music, wondering at the cause.

And there again, faintly commands may fill the evening air,
Or distant bugles at sunset to tell all to prepare
For the long sleep in prospect for this very special land,
Which served and satisfied its destiny from when first planned.

The Heavenly Battalion

There's a heavenly Battalion who sit at Gods right hand,
They wear a badge with torch and cross, with gear wheel all around.
They're noted for their raucous ways, and sense of humour, odd.
The angels are quite baffled by these lads chosen of God.

But under close inspection, it soon becomes quite clear,
Beneath the loud bonhomie, deep affection's always near,
They shared their youthful early life in ways known but by few,
And learned to love and live with zest as their comradeship grew.

And never, in remaining years, this bond so true and deep,
Could endure in the self-same way, to cherish and to keep.
For sharing with each other, all the worries and the joys,
Creating lasting brotherhood for those young, carefree boys.

And though time traversed slowly by, years taking their sad toll,
Those youthful memories lived on, until the final call.
Some were summoned at young age, for some, the passing slow,
But all remained, joined by that bond, created long ago.

So now they stand by heavens gate, greeting those to come,
And welcoming all those that they knew to Gods Reunion.
The heavens aren't so peaceful now, the harps are not so clear,
As a mighty chorus of "The Reds" assaults the angels' ears.

We need not grieve for those we knew, a brother or a chum,
For they will know the company of friends, and those to come.
But for a while, we who remain, stand silent and give thanks,
And know we'll meet again when called to join their heavenly ranks.

TeeCee

The Highland Bagpipe

The low burr of the bass drone blends with tenors, while the bag extends
To fill. Then, with a gentle squeeze the chanter chimes, and expertise
Borne of long hours of practise now comes forth at last to flower and show
The piper's skills, as fingers weave a magic pattern to achieve
A haunting musical display transporting spirit far away
To heather covered, rolling hills where bubbling burns and rippling rills
Cascade and sparkle on their way to waiting lochs, in fine display.

The piper's fingers deftly move, producing melodies that weave
And mix a rhythmic lilting potion, stirring yet again emotions
In the Celtic native breast, recalling proud historic tests
Of courage in the face of those who sought to subjugate, oppose
The Caledonian way of life. Provoking cruel years of strife
For fearless clansmen faithful to the Saltire Cross, where many true
And brave men died for that ideal to free them from the tyrant's heel.

And in the fastness midst the heights of mountains tall, majestic sights
Of towering peaks above the glens where stags rule in their

wild domain,
The pipes give their distinctive song with ghostly echo far along
A brooding, silent landscape there, and with that poignant, Highland Air,
Many homesick exiled men could wish that they were back again
To share the clear, untainted places of their homeland, turn their faces
Back to where their hearts still stay in that wild country far away.

And when at last they're laid to rest, no matter where, the pipes attest
To their proud ancestry and play laments to see them on their way;
While evening shadows drawing nigh and night enclosing starry skies,
The plaintive, clear seductive sound of Highland bagpipes all around
May just remind the listening ear of good times past, maybe a tear
Will briefly fall, as oft times when those magic fingers fly again,
Evoking thoughts of happy times spent in the land of Auld Lang Syne.

Not Forgetting ......

The Drummers

We bash away with joie de vivre, the noise we make, you'd not believe,
But it's our mission and our boast, that pipers will be deaf as posts
Before we end our drummers riff. So we'll proceed to bash and biff
Until we're satisfied that they can't hear a single note they play.
And then, content, we'll take a rest, but only for a moment, lest
They think that we are finally done, when we have only just begun!
So wipe away those pipers' tears, we'll be here yet for many years,
Giving you the beat you need, to stop you from increasing speed!

The Memorial

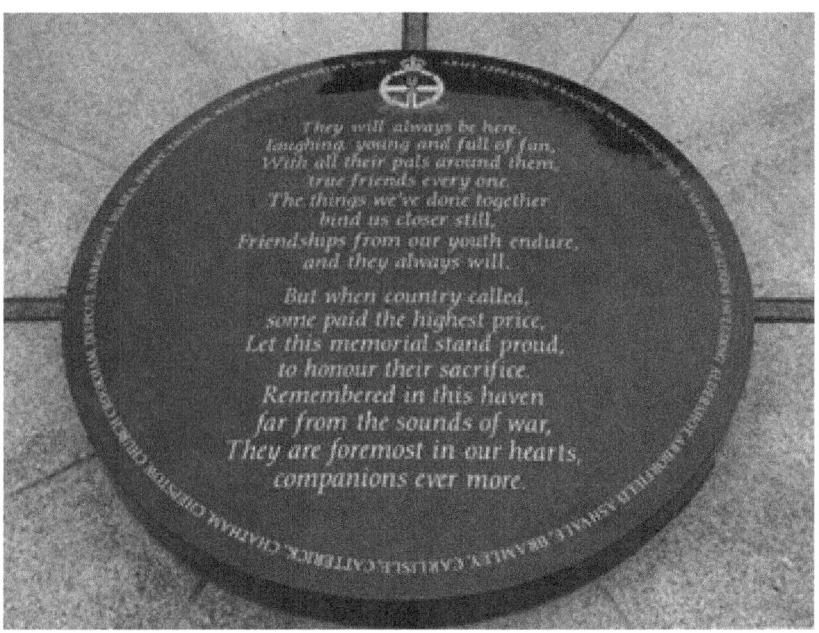

It stands in the shade of a green woodland glade, tranquil, restful, a place of reflection;
While a stream running near, nature's melody, clear, is a setting for quiet recollection.
And here, at its heart, the stonemason's art commemorates boyhood ambition,
To enlist, train and learn, and then, having earned their place, follow their chosen vocation.

This circle of stone tells of 'Boy's Schools', now flown into history's yellowing pages,
Of young boys' transitions to skilful technicians, through eras of momentous changes.
Yet a building alone, whether timber or stone, was just an inanimate part
Of a fine learning place; the real soul was embraced by the youngsters who gave it that heart.

The names inscribed here total many long years of staunch service, in conflict and peace,
And with pride represents the thousands who went and forsook lives of comfort and ease.
But their deeds and careers over many long years bear a testimony of great truth,
That when they were trained, the military gained the finest examples of youth.

And those old boys, now gone, will forever live on in this cloistered and quiet sanctuary,
Though some that remain will return yet again, and remember times when all was very
Exciting and new on life's threshold, imbued with eager, supreme expectation,
Lifelong friendships were made, never fated to fade, rooted firm in that youthful foundation.

So, pause as you pass this place, sit, read each name that's chased into the stonework laid here.
Each one could tell stories of ordeals and glories that stem from a soldier's career,
But in the beginning, ere the losing and winning that all in a martial life know,
That solid direction was laid by instruction in how to live life and to grow
Into maturity, learn of truth, loyalty, and, above all, of honour, fair play.
Lessons which then turned those boys into men, and a debt we can never repay.

The Good Old Days (?)

We're the old farts with withering parts, whose service go's way, way back when
The buttons were brass, the SD was nasty and rough, buttoned up to our chins.
Our lives were spent cleaning and polishing, dreaming of leave: to get out was our thought,
But there was no respite, no time off, and despite dogged efforts, it all came to nought.

We were blancoing, bumping, and generally jumping about, always under inspection,
And trying to please, exploring each wheeze that would help in evading detection
Of some small omission, and given sufficient forewarning, we usually managed
To hide the transgression, evading detention to limit collateral damage!

And yes, it was rough, although, fair enough, we did not really know any better,
From our point of view, it was all that we knew, to be endured in the hope we would get a
Reprieve from this grind after some little time, having suffered the depths of despair,
Indeed it became rather better, much tamer, when we'd done some extra time there.

But those were the years when our military peers were the ones who had just fought a war,
No 'human rights' then, no time for thin skin, "no complaints", "keep your mouth shut", what's more,

If you stepped out of line, no RP's and no fine, it was "jankers", and, boy, did you suffer!
From the morn at first light through the noon to midnight, could you honestly feel any rougher?

But it all had to change, when the imminent danger of war had receded at last,
And there came the decision that from now conscription was ended, a thing of the past.
Of course, then, the methods of discipline always were numbered from that time and so
A less strict regime was envisaged. Was seen to work well, so the old ways must go.

But nevertheless there are those who confess that those old times were not all that bad,
And in so many ways they were much gentler days, and the standards of life that we had
Were far more civilised, as we now realise, looking back at those days far away.
That we needn't be envious, it's they who should envy us, in this "modern" world of today.

TeeCee

The Piper's Requiem

The Piper stood at Heaven's gates, his bagpipes by his side,
But hesitant to enter, although they were open wide.
An angel chancing to pass by, paused, and made this demand,
"Are those a weapon of some kind that you hold in your hand?".
The Piper groaned, "A Sassenach!" As it became quite clear
That they were present everywhere, they even had them here!

"They were regarded as such, long ago", he then replied,
"But always made such harmonies that ever will abide
With images of heather clad hillsides with rippling burns,
Which every native Scotsman in his heart secretly yearns".
And gently coaxing out a melody his fingers wove
A highland air so exquisite, a song of peace and love.

And as he played, it seemed there was an echo distantly,
Until he was aware of other pipes in harmony,
And into view came highland pipers playing, by the score;
He recognised his old comrades, and then, so many more
That he had played a farewell for so many years long gone,
Who came, prepared to welcome him, his race now finally run.

For though their mortal span is over, pipers will transcend
This life, their spirit wings to where we cannot comprehend,
A place reserved for them somewhere in heaven's paradise,
Where chanters play quite easily, and drones are so precise.
Where reeds are perfect at all times and neither flat nor sharp,
And in this part of heaven, you will NEVER hear a harp.

So never fear, good Piper, you may now lay down and rest,
In knowledge that your friends considered you the very best
Example of what any man in this life can attain,
And truthfully will say that they won't see your like again,
You leave a space in people's lives but will forever be
One of God's heavenly pipers in celestial harmony.

TeeCee

The Roll Call

The roll call grows as countless years go by,
Some go too soon, while some, death's weary wait defy;
And now that all those things recalled inevitably decline,
It seems that we who remain, are left to wither on the vine.

But that is the way of life, as with all who have gone before,
And we, when ultimately existing in this life no more,
Can only hope that some token, mark or symbol of our worth
Will occupy a place, recording our brief time on this earth.

The passing presence of this turbulent, youthful tide
Must surely leave an echo in the fabric of the space we occupied,
While we, wherever destined to eventually be
May rest in satisfied, quiet repose for all eternity.

The Roll Call 2

The roll is called and once again we all become aware
That some old comrades will no longer come to join us there.
It is the price we all must pay as age and health decline,
Yet always seems unfair when some depart before their time.

We're told old soldiers never die, they only fade away,
But that is in the mortal self, by physical decay,
In memory and vivid recollection there's no sign
Of truth in that old oft repeated military rhyme.

While we who now remain can still bring those old friends to mind,
They will not 'fade away' to us, who now are left behind,

The opposite is true because of past times that we shared,
And so it will endure while there are those of us who care.

TeeCee

Two Minutes

Patiently they waited. Stood. The young, the old, the great and good,
Listening for the signal toll which marked eleven hours, then all
Was hushed, even the very birds refrained to sing, no sound was heard
Save rustling motion of a breeze disturbing the autumnal trees;
Of movement, motion, little - none. A scene set seemingly in stone.

And thousands, with heads bowed in thought, and some recalling battles fought
In long years past, with memories burned of comrades who did not return.
While those too young to know the pain and loss of war waited, remained
In patient vigil by their side, supporting those who did survive,
Respecting this, their pilgrimage to honour those from war's mad rage.

The seconds passed by, one by one, and bandsmen's instruments that shone
And glinted in the morning light, reflecting images in bright
Relief, prepared to play and sound as time came finally around
To end this brief but poignant pause in busy life, remembering wars,
And hoping peace would finally reign, no more the tears, the grief, and pain.

With every year this ceremony is held, we can but pray that the
Leaders of these earthly lands can find a way to understand
That war is simply not the way to settle disagreement. They
Have in their power the means for all to live in peace, and never fall
Into those ways of pain and death. But what's the chance?......

Don't hold your breath ……..

TeeCee

Us

We're better off than normal folks,
Behind wisecracks and those bad jokes
We've heard so many times before,
There hides a fact we can't ignore,
That deep within our psyche there's
A real sincerity that cares.

It stems from shared days long ago,
When we learned to live and show
Consideration to our friends,
Showing care that just transcends
The rough and ready bold façade
We showed, while masking true regard.

It's partly why, and to this day,
Pretending, (in a friendly way!)
We treat our mates with false disdain,
Yet if distressed we feel their pain,
For this concern stems from our past,
And learned and earned, forever lasts.

So we are fortunate indeed
To be part of that dying breed
Who, by discipline subjected,
Found in turn that we respected
All our pals who shared those ties,
And formed a bond that never dies.

TeeCee

We, of this Group

Of all the seventy thousand-odd who passed through our school gates
How many now know of this site - of their old Boy's-School mates?
We few, we gallant few, we band of brothers gathered here,
Dispensing words of wisdom, spreading bonhomie and cheer,
Keep up that spirit that we shared those many years ago,
Maintaining links that are so swiftly lost, carelessly so.

Yes, there are those who never want to be reminded now
Of their three years spent there, unhappily, yet still somehow,
It surely wasn't all gloom and doom and unremitting hell,
We did have great times, didn't tales, and we like to tell
Of escapades and episodes that stay in fond recall,
Like boxing matches, films and dances in the old Camp Hall?

For now we can forget the bull and bullies that we knew,
It's time to wear those spectacles of rosy tinted hue,
And spread the word to those who still recall with some distaste
Their time at Arborfield Boys School, who left in such great haste,
Not wanting ever to go back to memories best forgotten,
For them, three years which they regard as lost, wasted and rotten.

But now, when looking at those distant days of long ago,
It seems a shame that those who hated it are seemingly so
Bitter that they lose a certain essence of their youth,

Times that they ought to cherish as the years They learnt the truth
Of what living was all about, extremes, the highs, the strife,
And left, armed with the attitudes that served us well, for life.

So we will hopefully continue adding commentary
To all the every day events when happening, that we see,
And give opinion, good or bad, to all who wish to read,
For in our membership lies great experience, skill and deeds
And maybe, through the eyes that have observed more than most men,
Advance considered points of view to make us think again.

TeeCee

Whither "Boy's School"

There's a place just south of Reading in Berkshire's leafy lanes,
Where the builders ply their trade for all to see,
And the houses will be rising while the tractors and the cranes
Churn the ground beneath their wheels industrially.

In the midst of this chaotic scene, two pillars starkly wait,
Red brick, joined by an arch with torches there,
Proclaiming proudly of the boys who passed between their gates,
Into a life of comradeship and care.

They wait, on guard, like sentinels as 'progress' blunders in,
A barrier to hold the past in place,
Defending all the memories of things that once had been,
Against the march of time and mankind's race.

But nought will still the sands of time as through the glass they flow,
Their staunch defence will soon be overcome,
The symbols of our youth may vanish in the evening's glow,
A sacrifice to hunger for new homes.

The Garden, tended carefully, will soon be swept away,
The last remaining symbol of the past,
Replaced by flats and houses and young children at play,
All evidence of past memories laid to waste.

But memories can't be destroyed as buildings surely can,
And Old Boys will remember constantly

The times when they were young, strong men, fit to fight and fight again,
A band of brothers, facing life, carefree.

And, years from now the residents may think they hear a noise
Of marching feet, or distant bugle blow,
The skirl of pipes, the myriad sounds of thousands of young boys,
Who came to live those many years ago.

So in this ever changing world, when the past seems to have died,
The independent spirit does still thrive,
The vivid recollections still imbue the soul with pride,
And "Boys School" in its MEN will stay alive.

TeeCee

Airs on a bed spring

So if you will, survey the scene, some twenty youths, young, fit and lean,
In evening ritual engaged with never ending battle, waged
Against demands of those that rule that all must gleam within the school,
And so, employing rag and brush, with bumper, endless pull and push.

Accompanying this industry, the wooden wireless tirelessly
Is pumping out the Rock 'n Roll, motivating one and all
To greater efforts at their toil, lest they should weaken, or recoil
From burnishing the bucket bright, as on they labour through the night.

But, of a sudden all is changed, the labours cease, divorced, estranged,
Expectancy pervades the place, and all now pause, then turn and face
The one whose sphincter rules the roost at half-past-eight, when he lets loose
The blasts in two or three-four time, controlled, and in its way, sublime.

For this is Fred, whose lithe young frame supports that which has gained him fame
And triumph as the one so smart, exponent of the artful fart,
(A claim not gained by easy means, much practice with the aid of beans

Consumed at mealtimes was required, to reach the standard he desired!)

But now, as his moment arrives, young Fred, with pants removed, contrives
To point his anus to the skies, as now, all conversation dies
Awaiting the appropriate piece to demonstrate his expertise,
The hush descending o'er the room, anticipating flatulent boom.

At last the intro now begins, and "Tutti Frutti"'s strains now spins
Around the gathered throng, as Fred shouts "Ready!" Lifting from the bed,
His fundament, preparing to impress his audience now, who
Await in fascinated awe to witness music in the raw.

It starts. He's there right on the beat as methane whistles o'er the sheets,
Reverberating through the place as C sharp, E flat takes their place
In perfect rhythm to the tune and, as applause then fills the room,
He finishes his master class with rhapsody straight from the arse.

And these days there'd be no surprise, they'd praise our Fred up to the skies
Should he enter a talent show, for, as we all too rightly know
That most X Factor stuff is crap, he'd walk it, for this talented chap
Was one alone, (but one small note – not pleasant when he cleared his throat!

Yet Another Goodbye

We, who trod that road together many years ago,
Living, sharing all the full and boisterous days that so
Epitomised the youthful spirit that bound us so close,
Saw us tied in brotherhood through best times and the worst.

Then when we went our separate ways, exploring pastures new,
Little did we think, consider that the comrade who
Had been our close companion for three years through thick and thin
In course of time would reappear to share our lives again.

Yet, as the years elapse and we grow older, thoughts return
Increasingly, and often then our inner spirit yearns
To re-establish what we had, for we found out, as men,
That what we had was special, though we didn't know it then.

And that road that we trod together, many years ago,
Has now become our precious memory lane, which we follow,
Recalling things through half forgotten, rekindled recollection,
Of adventures and friendships, oft with wry but fond affection.

But when one of our number comes to bid a sad farewell,
We are diminished, each and every one of us as well,
For that tie which we carried from those days in memory,
Means as one goes we lose a little of that entity.

So they will always be recalled by those who shared their youth,
When what was learned first and foremost was loyalty and truth,
They'll live on in fond memory, secure in hearts and minds
Of all those many friends who shared those happy, youthful times.

TeeCee

ARMY APPRENTICES' SCHOOL, ARBORFIELD. APPRENTICE SERJEANTS. NOVEMBER, 1957

A/Sjt. G. R. Laker, R. Milcburn, D. J. Batchelor, B. C. Wells, C B Moss, J H Lee, J. T. Huggett, L. Wells, N. Rowlands
A/Sjts. A. R. Watson, C. R. Nattress, A. R. Cook, P. D. Anderson, F. Ede, R. Mansbridge, L. H. Chicken, R. J. Runacres
A/Pipe Major M. Blean, A/CSM. M. R. Nash, A/CSM. J. R. Dickson, A/RSM. J. Massie, Colonel J. R. Cole, A/CSM. D. D. McNish, A/CSM. K. G. Andrews,
(Commandant)
A/Sjt. F. T. Freeman, A/Drum Major A. Church

"A" SQUAD, JUNIOR COMPANY, ARMY APPRENTICES SCHOOL, ARBORFIELD
INTAKE 1965 A, 12th JANUARY 1965 to 15th APRIL, 1965

Part Two: Regular Army Life

Arte et Marte

Gold Lightning barb and Silver Steed, the Crown and Globe enclosing
The opening Scroll, proclaiming REME - simple, yet imposing.
This is the badge so proudly worn by members of the Corps
Which keeps the army on the move, prepared to go to war.
Yet, battle honours there are none despite its long existence,
For it has been in every action, giving its assistance;

And if all of these engagements were actually listed,
It would be (probably) the longest standard that's existed.

Now there are those who claim that REME personnel don't fight,
And this misconception must, in all justice, be put right,
For, lacking military expertise, there's no hope of promotion,
As 'Soldier First and Tradesman Second', is the REME notion.
For, when in action things look bad, the frontline combat soldier
Knows REME men will be fighting with them, shoulder to shoulder
Until the battle has been won, or till the danger fades,
And then assume their primary role, returning to their trades.

So REME soldiers of today continue this tradition,
Supporting, as has always been the case, without condition,
Prepared to do whatever is required to aid success,
Regardless of the toll that they may suffer, or distress
That might be part of helping out in whatsoever role
That they may be required to fill, to answer duty's call;
One thing is sure, no matter what is asked of them to do,
Tradition's always safe with REME lads, they'll see it through.

TeeCee

Aden

On the West of the Indian Ocean, on the bit that's just by the Red Sea,
There's a place that was known as a main cornerstone of the Empire by Royal Decree.
In most schoolboys first stamp collections it was usually on the first page,
With "ADEN" writ large at the top with King George in the corner - royal patronage.

It was not the best posting for many, hot and humid, with too many flies,
A rocky terrain that made driving a pain and a smell that you couldn't disguise.
But nevertheless, we had to confess compensations were there to be had,
And once reconciled to the local lifestyle, it wasn't all really that bad.

Life could be humdrum, though up country for some, it did get unpleasant at times,
And in the last year, there were not many tears when we left it forever behind.
Yet through years before many thousands endured this outpost of Imperial might
With determination and much perspiration, both ready and willing to fight.

But when the old sweats (and that term really fits!) from those barren rocks do congregate,
The lamp really swings as they recall the things that they shared with their old service mates,

And then, Steamer Point, the bazaars and that joint by the causeway, the hours of play
All come back to life as the chaps and their wives reminisce on those great, far-off days.

The duty-free shops, cheap cameras and watches and plentiful things with no charge
With short working days gave opportune ways to enjoy social life by and large.
So Elephant Bay and the Mermaid Club played a large part in the lives of us all,
With permanent sun and the servants to run things, while we played and just had a ball.

We climbed Shamsan's peak, though shattered and weak from exertion and nasty sunburn,
For 'twas written somewhere that If we got there, when we left, we would never return.
So," Insurance!", we thought, and decided it ought to be worthwhile, though rather insane
To repeat the chore, but it was worth being sure, so we got up and climbed it again!

All ships passing through, stopped off here, while the crew and the passengers headed ashore
To spend all their cash, and being quite rash with their money made all prices soar.
And so we waited till the ships had vacated their berths and the prices went down,
Then once more returned to the haunts that we learnt were the best and the cheapest in town.

The cheap booze and fags helped to ease time that dragged, ever slowly, it seemed, for two years,

For this dusty land of rocks, burning sand, could reduce strong men almost to tears,
But we made a stand in that forsaken land, for our masters decreed that we should,
And we must believe in these later years, that the things that we did were all good.

For some that went there would forever lie where they were rested, by comrades with care,
And In that foreign place it must not be a waste to think that they died needlessly there;
But what we did gain midst the heat and the pain, inhospitable climes and the strife,
Was a comradeship rare for all that were there, which has lasted for many, for life.

TeeCee

Barrack Room Humour

Barrack room humour is now dead and gone,
That which we bandied about and which shone
With a non - PC attitude, yet to invent,
Employed by us all with amusing intent.
It brightened our lives and sharpened our wits;
Frequently ribald, it kept us in fits
Of perpetual laughter in formative years
As we shared every day with our barrack room peers.
Occasionally subtle, but sometimes quite blunt
Used by some to demonstrate, and maybe flaunt
Their command of that jocular, odd repartee
That we used every day, so familiarly.

To those not acquainted with this kind of fun,
Which often seemed cruel and unkind to some,
The barbs of verbosity thrown in the air,
Appeared to them that we did not really care.
Yet nothing could be so far from what was meant,
The seemingly savage and cutting comment
Was in a strange way, but a form of reflection,
Of our brotherhood's way of showing affection.

And over the years as our lovers and wives
Have joined and become the main parts of our lives,
They realized in time, this was merely an act,
Concealing the plain, undeniable fact
That insults, derision, or sarcastic quip
Were merely disguising the close comradeship
That we had engendered in our younger days,
And then manifested itself in these ways.

It was just a sign of the way we lived then,
And never will be the case ever again,
For the impetus now is to seek great offence,
Ignoring the often underlying intent
At humour, misplaced now in this day and age
Of so-sensitive egos, ready to rage
At the merest suggestion of great provocation,
And seeking repayment, or some compensation.

So value those old days of simplicity,
When thoughts of contention or adversary,
Were alien to most of us, and day-to-day,
We merely desired to go our own way
Without fear of what others may just construe
To be slanderous, libelous, even though true.
Remember when we could just say what we mean,
And Barrack Room Humour reigned so supreme

TeeCee

Bill Millin, The Making of a Legend

On D-Day, Sixth of June, at dawn, a young man, destined to become
A legend in the coming years, suppressing all his natural fears,
Responded to his Chief's command and played his pipes along that strand
Of open beach in Northern France, well knowing that the laws of chance
Were firmly set against him there, as noise of battle filled the air.
And so, though seasick, wet and cold, he complied as he had been told.

Though he had previously explained, reminding Lovat of the change
Of orders from The High Command that pipers at the front were banned.
And Lovat, giving this some thought, contemplated that he ought,
As senior man, not make young Bill ignore an order, yet he still
Required our hero to perform to raise morale amid the storm
Of battle's turmoil, so said he, "An English law, it seems, to me,
And for the English this is meant, so as Scots soldiers, we're exempt!"

And play he did, so all around above the roar, the stirring sound
Of "Hielan' Laddie" cleft that din, repeated time and time again

To help his comrades in their fight to gain that ground, ignoring fright
And dread of instant, cold, cold death. He, summoning up his every breath,
Marched on, "Road to the Isles" now played, as Lovat's order he obeyed.

And so the legend here was born, of how he braved the lethal storm
Of fire and carnage, utter hell and then unscathed, lived on to tell
The story that, in later years, his erstwhile enemies appeared
To doubt their eyes, for this man clad in kilt was surely quite, quite mad!
So "Mad" became Bill's designation, and all because determination
To obey a direct order was his duty as a soldier!

So time has passed and swiftly flown, Bill now has bowed to fate and gone
To join his comrades at their rest who represented all the best
Of manhood in their natural prime who gave their lives before their time
Was due, to answer country's call. So now to venerate them all,
A fitting tribute should be found, recording courage so profound.

To mark this one historic act on that day, which was surely packed
With many deeds of worthy note, of lives laid down for dearly wrought

Success, a statue of this man, in highland kilt and pipes will stand
By that same beach to represent not just our Bill, but all who went
And gave their all to fight that day, some fated not to walk away,
Yet willingly, without reproach, revitalizing freedom's torch.

The freedoms that we now display, although not perfect, we may say,
Were never cheaply bought by those who recognizing danger, fought
To keep that which we hold so dear, (and take for granted now, I fear.)
Therefore, to keep these deeds in mind, this apt memorial will combine
The memory of Bill's epic walk on Sword Beach, midst the fire and smoke,
With all his comrades .He and they deserve this tribute, so let's pay
Whatever we feel they deserve in their great willingness to serve.

It may just be a modest sum, but can ensure that those who come
In future years will see and trace the moving history of this place,
And have a feeling or a sense of those dramatic, past events
Which shaped our history to this day, reminding us of those who lay
Their futures at the door of fate, some passing through, while others waited,
Fighting to ensure what we enjoy today so casually;

The right to free, peaceful expression, safe from alien, vile repression.

TeeCee

Bloggs Bogs

This is the tale of Private Bloggs, who hated cleaning out the bogs,
When room job lists were on the wall, he'd look, and then his face would fall
As he saw, from the job list numbered, he had once again been lumbered
With the most detested task, and though, in vain, he'd plead and ask
To be excused, 'twas no avail, and warned that should he try and fail
To clean them up, work any flankers, he'd be on perpetual jankers
Till his Passing out Parade – a threat, he knew, not idly made.

And so it came to pass that Bloggs was doomed, forever cleaning bogs,
No matter how he planned and plotted, he got permanently knotted
By his senior NCO's who had it in for him because
He had shown some independence with no subsequent repentance,
Certain to antagonize the powers-that-be, who realized
That this had to be nipped in the bud, for otherwise it really could
Mark the beginning of the end of discipline which all depends.

The moral of this story is, that if you get into a tizz
And try to go your separate way, there is a chance that you well may
Get more than you had bargained for, and find yourself with extra chores

That you had not anticipated, doing things you really hated,
Just because you, at the time, decided not to toe the line,
And suffered all the consequences of your military offences,
And guarantee ere it began, your whole career's gone down the pan!

TeeCee

Bombers Moon

"A bombers moon", and so it was, bright, riding in the sky,
We knew it meant that we would get a visit by and by.
The sirens wail, the clattering feet, the breathless, usual rush
To air raid shelters all close by, and then the deathly hush.
No sound now; sirens silenced. In candle's flickering light,
The shadows dancing on the walls; faces drawn and tight
With dread anticipation of sure impending doom,
The children tucked, snug in their cots, not knowing things to come.

It starts. The distant buzz of engines growing louder still,
The tell-tale throb, which marks the start of hell, begins to fill
The senses, as the nerves grow taut, anticipating, dreading,
Then distant guns start to confront the threat, suddenly shredding
Night-time blackness, muzzle flashes lancing up, defying,
And searchlight beams grope through the smoky fog, seeking and prying.
Their quest, to strip the foe of darkness, cloaking mean intention,
Revealing all in nakedness, its vulnerable dimension.

But now we feel vibration through the ground and air approaching,
As distant wails of missiles on our senses soon encroaching,
Till suddenly, with scream on scream our world is filled with thunder,
As close - too close, they pass us by, to leave us all to wonder

What lies outside the door of our safe underground protection,
Will things be just the same or will life take a new direction?
Until the all-clear sounds, then we're just going to have to wait,
To find out if our house still stands or what has been its fate.

And so, eventually we hear the all-clear sirens moan,
Emerging in the cool fresh air, we see what has been done,
And carry on as best we can, though tired through lack of sleep,
Working in our common task, to win through and to keep
Our spirits high, determined still to succeed at all costs,
Never to admit our struggle could be somehow lost;
To try to overcome and keep the enemy at bay,
For now, we have survived again to fight another day.

TeeCee

Chuff Charts

They were invented by National Servicemen who looked forward to the great day
When they could return to the families they yearned for, from which they'd been dragged rudely away
For two years (and occasionally more for some) from a good life of comfort and ease,
To an awful existence of starvation, poverty – at least that was what some had believed.
So, mostly in the Spartan surroundings of huts which had survived two world wars,
They devised a means of bringing their dreams of escape, (in their minds) to the fore.

Arming themselves with some paper and pencils, or paintbox with crayons and pens,
They drew out a plan for each single man, of the days that elapsed to the end
Of this sentence to which they had been rudely subjected, by Governments and solemn decree,
Producing a chart of a calendar sort which counted down days left to be
Served of eventual service before their final demobilization,
When they'd hand in their kit, leg it sharpish and get, with relief, back to "civilianisation!"

Our motives, though different to theirs, without doubt, did at least have a common intent,
We could, at least, mark each day as it passed away, bringing nearer the time when we went
On Leave, be it Easter or Christmas, or better, the six-week long Summer recess,

When we were so free, reverting almost to be civvies – well, practically more or less!
When our mates would say to us, almost each day, "Blimey, when do you go back?"
And we would just grin, knowing that soon, again, we'd be getting our workwear unpacked.

So these charts which were always scribed with "DTD" - our shorthand for the 'Days To Do'
Varied from crudely drawn to some artistic form which could grace some Art Galleries too;
Highly decorated, admired and feted, prominently placed on proud display,
They still served their purpose to remind and serve us, as we crossed our young lives away.
And that didn't matter, we were young and had a full lifetime ahead of us then,
But now it's behind me, I'm not really so keen to Chuff Chart what I've got left, again!

TeeCee

Comradeship

"No man is an island." T'was what the poet said,
And there's no doubt that man without friends might as well be dead.
But we, who in our early days lived close without the choice,
Contained in meagre living space, had less cause to rejoice
Than others, who, at home with family in their privacy
Could ignore fellow men, in their complete totality.

But now that time has slipped away, and seen in retrospect,
That, far from being deprived, we found we'd gained in one respect,
By living with the other men in close proximity,
We learned consideration and I think we'd all agree
That the virtue known as 'Comradeship' was in our hearts, and who
Could not now envy us this precious gift, now known by few.

The virtue gained by us this way, when in our youth and prime,
Is reason why that comradeship has stood the test of time,
It shows most, when old servicemen congregate in any form,
Be it here on our own corner, or even on the phone
The old concerns are always there, the empathy is plain,
And that old comradeship is there, to help and aid again.

So in this modern age, when certain words are rarely heard,
And 'Comradeship' and 'Loyalty' are thought to be absurd,
We should feel privileged that we once held these facets dear,
And though the current order seems to be to mock and sneer,

There is one thing that we do know, t'would surely be the case
That with more comradeship, this world would be a better place.

TeeCee

"ECE'S"

The lad, who as an Ece trains, is credited with superior brains,
Because his diagnostic skills, require him sometimes to fulfil
A knotty task, that's sight unseen, where theory counts, a mind that's keen,
And razor sharp, so he can tell where problems lie, and almost smell
A faulty loom, or diode, duff, armed with his wiring diagram rough,
He squints at multi coloured wires, stays on the job and never tires,
Until success has been secured, discomfort, tiredness, all endured
To keep the Ece's, in their grace, on Gods right hand - their rightful place !

(But as an afterthought, be fair, VM's also deserve their share
Of credit. And the allied trades, whose skills and muscle also made
The REME what it is today, the finest force, far and away,
So all you craftsmen, take a bow, you made the Corps what it is now !)

TeeCee

Epitaph for Afghanistan

Yet still the toll is rising, and muted drums beat, low,
While more young lives are squandered by those who do not know
Or seem to care, for they, naïve and blind, were never ever wont to see
The sights and sounds of battle, and man's inhumanity.

For glory, there is none, save in romantic poets prose,
The shining deeds of derring-do which vanquish all our foes
Are mostly works of fiction, the truth will never sell,
Known all too vividly by those who lived this man-made hell.

Of bravery there is no doubt as with each dawning day
A soldier knows full well that he could be the one who pays
The price that many have before, and no doubt will, again,
Yet discipline and duty means he will endure the pain.

For pain it is to see his comrades fall, to hear their cries,
As desperately he binds their wounds in anguished bid to try
To staunch their life-blood as it flows, staining the very ground,
That they came to protect, defend, by oath of loyalty bound.

Yet even as they fight to help this wild, benighted nation,
Observing all the carnage, they must feel the desperation
That others armies felt in many decades past, as they
In their turn, tried to show these warring peoples peaceful ways.

It is a soldier's lot to perform many thankless tasks,
And without question he will do as senior leaders ask.

But they who lead must also do their duty to their men,
And give them respite when a futile campaign is in vain.

The time has surely come when truth and reason will prevail,
And no more young lives squandered as valiantly they fail
To carry out the tasks that politicians glibly frame,
They now deserve to come home without ignominy or shame.

TeeCee

Heroes

Heroes. Do they deserve that name? Was it for glory that they came
To serve their country? "No!" they'd say, t'was for the prospect to obey
And answer to their nation's need for young, fit youth to take the lead
In causes just; defend the weak, wherever tyrants try to seek
To force their will upon all those who yearn for freedom from their cause.

But call them heroes? All they'd see is journalists' hyperbole,
Just serving, trying to bring peace to those who suffer; work to cease
Their misery, make life again a worthwhile thing, and free from pain
Of prejudice, an end to strife. Return Gods given gift of life
That's each and every person's right to dignity, a future bright.

These lofty ideals, they may claim, may not quite set their hearts aflame,
Rather, through their daily role when in support or on patrol,
They aid and help their comrades there, to carry out their duties, where
Dangers lurk and menace waits at every corner, door or gate,
With nerves stretched taut at every turn when omnipresent fear returns.

So are they heroes? That's to say, not in the more accepted way

Of glory hunting men of steel, dashing, wanting to appeal
To public gaze, be held in awe, strong silent guardians of the law.
These are average common folk who like to laugh, enjoy a joke,
But when it's time to pay the price, they'll freely make that sacrifice.

For after all is said and done, to conquer fear and carry on,
Advancing into the unknown, even when all help is gone,
Is heroism beyond reproach, and we should honour those who touch
Our hearts by their example bright, who surely now have earned the right
To stand among our heroes all, who boldly answered duty's call.

TeeCee

Home at Last

He's home at last, a mother's son, a fine young man, his duty done,
Yet not for him the fond embrace, a loving kiss, a smiling face
Or cries of joy to laugh and cheer the safe return of one so dear,
It is his lot to show the world a soldier's fate as flags unfurl
And Standards lower in salutation, symbols of a grateful nation.

Sombre now, the drum beats low, as he is carried, gentle, so
As if not to disturb his rest, by comrades, three and three abreast
Who now, as quiet orders sound, they, one by one then move around
To place him in the carriage decked with flowers in calm and hushed respect,
Preparing for the sad, slow ride through silent crowds who wait outside.

So the warrior now returns to native soil and rightly earns
The great respect to one so young, though sadness stills the waiting throng,
While flowers strew the path he takes, as the carriage slowly makes
A final turning to allow the veterans standing there to show
The soldiers pride, a silent, mute, proud and respectful last salute.

Yet, while onlookers stand and see the simple, moving ceremony,

There is a home, a place somewhere, where sits a waiting, vacant chair,
And one great yawning empty space in someone's heart, no last embrace
To bid a final, fond farewell to one who will forever dwell
In love and cherished memory, a Husband, Son, eternally.

And we who see should not forget that in this soldier's final debt
And sacrifice for duty's sake, it is the loved ones who must take
The hurt, to bear as best they can, and face a future lesser than
The one they dreamed in bygone years, now to regard with bitter tears,
Reflecting, as time intervenes, on thoughts of how it might have been.

But in their grief there's quiet pride that loved ones bravely fought and died
Believing in a worthy goal which helps give solace, and consoles
By knowing that the loss they bear is shared by all our peoples where
In gratitude, their names will be forever honoured, guaranteed
To be remembered and enshrined, beyond the shifting sands of time.

Lights Out, At Rest

The notes so plaintively proclaim the fast approaching dark domain
Of eventide, the end of day, when all things must be put away
For quiet repose, to pause, to rest, to cease the labours that invest
The daily round that all endure, until a new day dawns once more.

Yet in a life of duty, care, a time must come when all must bear
The truth that finally all things end, and we must lose a faithful friend,
A friend whose life was spent, indeed, in answer to his country's need
Of loyal and long service, true, an inspiration, through and through.

So rest, old soldier, duty done, your race at last in this life, run,
A lifetime's service for all others, comrades close as any brothers;
No-one could have given more, with honour lived, respected for
The standards kept and held with pride, now take your rest, in peace, abide.

TeeCee

Numbers and Initials

The very first thing we had to remember
When taking the shilling, was our army number.
On pain of reprisals too painful to bear,
We had to recite it, like learning a prayer.

Without numbers, the army would cease to exist,
There are millions of them, too long here to list.
They cover all aspects of military life,
We encountered them daily, yes, numbers were rife.

Two-five-two was the one to make you feel blue,
And coupled with letters, DRO's one and two.
And what about Army Form FMT3
When you've just bent the end of your new ARV?

And, beloved of REME, the Ten-Forty-Five,
Plus the Ten-Forty-Three, (first-class licence to skive!)
Your life was mapped out on AB 64,
Parts One and Part Two, these you couldn't ignore.

For without them, you didn't stand much of a chance
Of receiving your pay, so they were, on balance
A real necessity, and something to treasure,
One of few forms you could cherish with pleasure.

These are some examples of what we endured,
Like AWOL, this happened if you went overboard,
Or not even that, if you ran out of time,
By failure to make Twenty-Three-Fifty-Nine!

Yet GOC's, C-IN-C's, CRÈME's and such,

To civilians, they might as well be double Dutch,
But to squaddies, well versed in this strange, shorthand speak,
It saves explanation and keeps the mystique!

TeeCee

Old Soldier

Every inch the soldier in the scarlet coat he's wearing,
Ramrod straight and upright, with true military bearing,
He's seen a lot of changes since he joined as a boy,
Some were for the soldier's good, but most gave him no joy.

Titles changed, no longer was "War Office" deemed 'PC',
Some thought it was aggressive and too damned military:
Instead they came up with the name, the "Ministry of Defence",
Which, now run by civilians, should have been "Intransigence".

They stonewalled all requests by servicemen, both young and old,
Because their bible was a balance sheet, therefore they told
All those who came to them for sympathetic consultation,
That nothing could be spared, denied appeal, consideration.

Although by their incompetence and lack of understanding
Of basic needs for which the services required funding,
They squandered untold millions on futile exercises,
While starving the armed forces of more life saving devices.

Yet, soldiers have forever employed skilful enterprise
To meet adversity, and readiness to improvise
In face of danger from their enemies, or so-called friends,
To minimise the damage and maintain a strong defence.

One unforeseen advantage that this lack of care inspired,
By civil servants, and the politicians; people, tired
Of the injustices which left them quite appalled,
Saw through the hypocrites excuses, and at last, rebelled.

So now, at long last, Kiplings verses don't really ring true,
At least regarding public attitudes, they seldom do,
For, thanks to politicians who have mostly never served,
The forces now have got the understanding they deserve.

And that old soldier will be able to stand up and say
That he was fortunate to live and see at last the day
When those who fight to keep us safe from all whom wish us ill,
Have admiration and support, but most of all, lasting goodwill!

I wonder now, how many lads on leave, have heard the crack,
"Well hello mate, on leave again? When are you going back?"
Though, come to think of it, some habits are ingrained, prolonged,
So, on reflection I won't hold my breath for all that long!

TeeCee

Pegasus. Ancient and Modern

Born in mythology, riding the sky, the mount of Bellerophon, see how he flies!
Noble and fearless, surmounting the clouds, he wings over the earth with spirit unbowed,

No better emblem could be so designed to personify he who himself has combined
These qualities matched by his passion to win yet face all that comes with a wink and a grin.
For this airborne fighter is the soldier who flies into action, and bent on achieving surprise,
Arrives from above, and, trusting his all to some chord and a shroud to cushion his fall,
Will overcome those who may stand in his way, for he is determined to fight and obey
The command he is given and never will fail to give of his best, to defeat and prevail.

And proudly he wears the distinctive beret, not red, but maroon which he earned in a way
That no average person could ever achieve, for selection is hard, and many do leave
Before gaining the wings, which proudly acclaim that this person has endured the hardship and pain
Which lesser men forswear for comfort and leisure, unable to equal this warrior's measure.
The names that resound down the years they bestride are bywords for courage and soldierly pride,
Recalling tenacious engagements and more, illustrious battles and deeds by the score
Of sacrifice, guts and endurance supreme, now marked in the

pages of history, seen
By the new generations who admire these men who have fought and succeeded, again and again.

And when, duty done, they obey fate's last call to start that short journey for the final fall,
There'll be no reserve chute, no static lines there, for this time the DZ's located somewhere
In the heavens, where comrades who've journeyed before, from Arnhem, Goose Green, Normandy, many more,
Will welcome them in as they queue at the gates, while the heavenly jumpmaster patiently waits
To issue them once again with their own wings, so they will be free to continue the things
That they did in a lifetime of service to others, accompanied by their own select band of brothers.
For they are the 'Paras', proud, brave and daring, with a motto so apt, "Ready for Anything"

TeeCee

Rece Mechs

They're not what you'd call regimental – well, not in a military way,
And likely as not they'd be other than what you'd expect in the army today.
Shiny boots and smart turnout – forget it! Shaggy haircuts are likely the norm,
Perfect strangers to blanco and bullsh*t, no way will these soldiers conform.
There's not much that can be done with them, it's best to just leave well alone
And let them adjourn in the hope they'll return when the urge has died for them to roam.
It's also a quite good idea when on exercise out in the field
To lock up the stores, and bolt all the doors and keep all the good kit concealed.
For these masters of improvisation will liberate what's not secured,
With innocent faces and all signs and traces of larcenous action obscured.

They can be a pain in the rear end – independent and barely controlled,
But when things get bad, then everyone's glad that they're easily worth their weight in gold.
'Cos when bogged down right in the action and prospects are not looking bright,
They'll be there when they're needed – no call goes unheeded, and stay and continue to fight
Till they've got the result that they strove for, succeeded again with a grin,
And with cheerful wave to another they've saved, they're off

on their travels again.
So all Reccy Mechs of the REME, it's time to stand up, take a bow,
For without you, the army ain't moving until you're there, giving a tow;
And, rightly, you think you're the chosen, for when they're all stuck in a truck,
They'll all give a cheer as you reappear, before again, slinging your hook!

TeeCee

Red Arrows

High summer. Azure tinted sky. Clouds of cotton wool float high
Above, in limpid haze, while corrugated heat waves craze
The far horizon. All is still, yet in the waiting host, a thrill
Of expectation keens the senses, eager, watchful; the silence is
So intense, and so profound as ears strain, listening for the sound
Which heralds yet again the sight of nine winged messengers, a flight
In perfect line, consummate skill, preparing to amaze and thrill.

But yet, the stillness is unbroken, a question hangs above, unspoken,
"Will they come?" or "Are they late?" When, in reply a sudden great
Thunderous sound explodes, then fades, invading ears of those that wait,
As if from nowhere, they appear, and from the crowd a lusty cheer
For these knight-errants of the air who, with their scarlet chargers dare
To fulfil deeds of flying skill and give the throng their eager fill
Of dazzling flair and bold precision, an aerial gymnastic vision.

They climb, ascending in formation, each one holding to its station,
Almost touching so it seems, yet every one who forms this

team
Is practiced in this aerial game, so, welded to some unseen frame
They loop and soar, the coloured trails of smoke behind their crimson tails
Etching the red, white and the blue across the sky as they go through
The exquisite aerial ballet that they devised; flying displays
Delighting all the earthbound folk and quiet pride that they invoke.

For these are our own native sons and daughters who have undergone
The training and the discipline to gain this accolade and win
A place in this elite formation, won unstinted admiration
For their exploits far and wide, retained affection and our pride
In demonstrating to our eyes that they are masters of the skies,
Ruling supreme in their domain, and gaining the respect again
Of others who were born to grace the freedom of this open space.

And we stand, awestruck, marvelling, as these young aviators fling
Their painted darts across the sky, creating fountain-heads with high
Precision, artistry in smoke, dispersing, gradually to cloak
Their final act, as they swoop low in their goodbye to end the show,
Departing, leaving all whom saw their exploits, feeling the warm glow
Of knowing they'd been entertained to highest standards, and had gained

Some memory from images upon the sky, the supreme stage.

But let us pause in quiet reflection and bring to mind the recollection
Of the price that may be paid to bring this aerial parade
Of skill and daring to our lives There have been those whose sacrifice
Has been the charge, the toll to pay in duty; therefore every day
That this team go into the skies, perform before our awestruck eyes,
The spirit of the ones now gone will fly, for-mating, as they had done
In those years past with skill and verve, their lasting epitaph deserved.

TeeCee

Sand in my Shoes

I often reflect on my soldiering years, and think of the best ones that I would most choose
And after much soul-searching consideration, I think it was when I had sand in my shoes.
Yes, it was a quite stench ridden sweaty old posting with not much provided except fags and booze,
But that was real soldiering, bloody and painful, yet memories are pleasant of sand in my shoes.

No time for the bull or square bashing in Blighty, no long kit inspections to while away time,
When cleaning your weapons, you sure as hell meant it, you didn't just do it to improve the shine.
And water was something you found in a hole in the middle of nowhere, so careful to use,
You drank it quite sparingly, shaved not so often in those days when I had that sand in my shoes.

Sentry-go in those old circular sangars, nerves quite on edge as you wandered about,
Look at 'em long enough, bushes start moving, you're finger's on trigger and ready to shout
For a password, to stand-to, then - Gawd! –it's a camel! So easy, out there to get all confused,
You might look a fool when you're on active service, so damned trigger happy with sand in your shoes.

But when daylight fades and the darkness envelops the wadis and jebels in velvety shade,
There comes a sensation of deep profound wonder, to look at the heavenly starry brocade

That spreads out above, beyond the horizon a mixture of dark blue and purple tinged hues,
And studded with diamonds, all sharp, brightly shining, momentarily forgetting the sand in my shoes.

The streaks of the shooting stars etching their paths in a seemingly endless flight fill the night sky,
And glinting, the winking beads of the far galaxies fill one with wonder and identify
Those far constellations which are so familiar when we're back at home where we look up and choose
The North Star for our bearings, but here, there's no sign of it, searching in vain with the sand in our shoes.

And that's my most treasured remembrance of those days, sweating and soldiering 'neath eastern skies,
Not the flies and the bedbugs, and little black scorpions that lay in your boots to give you a surprise.
No, the heavenly beauty of Gods own creation, when far, far away from all man-made abuse
Will stay with me long after all else has faded of times when I walked there with sand in my shoes.

TeeCee

Silent Valley

In the shadow of the peaks on South Arabia's dusty plain
A roofed gate stands, reminder of a half-forgot campaign,
When once again our servicemen were called upon to fight,
Defending and protecting, (we were told) Great Britain's might.

But not forgotten, ever, by those who served out there,
Remembering the sweat and stench, the never-ending glare
Of unremitting scorching sun and blessed, welcome relief
As night descended, giving respite from remorseless heat.

Those gates are silent sentinels, through which there is revealed
The graves of those who rest here, in this arid alien field.
They lie, not in the green fields of their rightful native land,
Where flowers bloom and gently wave, by gentle breezes fanned.

Instead, the hard, unyielding ground, volcanic, harsh and dry,
Encloses those who, in the end, came here to fight and die.
Surrounded by gaunt, lofty spires, all stark against the light
Brooding guardians of our countrymen by day and night

They are condemned by history to occupy this earth,
Never able to return to the dear country of their birth,
No loved ones to attend them, no tears will ever fall
On the plain, white simple headstones that lie within this wall.

But this is how it was, in all but very recent years,
And there is consolation knowing willing volunteers
Care for and tend these places sacred to the memory

Of those who gave their lives in the pursuit of liberty.

And not just here in Silent Valley, many other lands
Are hosts to British servicemen and women, where there stand
Headstones engraved with names of those whose fate was finally sealed
To stay forever in the corner of some foreign field.

TeeCee

Silent Witnesses

Stark, mute, they stand there, row on row, each one a testament to show
The folly of man's foolish pride; the arrogantly thrown aside
Ideas of tranquil co-existence, trampled by some blind insistence
Of a lust for power and glory, peace forsaken for war's fury.

Yet also they proclaim the right to take up arms and lead the fight
To those who have such mean regard for humankind and seek reward
In violent act, barbaric deed inspired by avaricious greed,
Which humane spirit must suppress in like response by armed duress.

And so these simple markers stand, quite unassuming, almost bland
In unpretentious plain design, regardless of rank, a benign
And honest statement to us all that in death, man-made titles fall
Into inconsequential form and matter not when life is shorn.

But in their purpose they excel, in simple narrative they tell
Of someone who, in honour bound commitment, died, and in this ground
They lie, a noble company, distinguished in their equity
Of gallant conduct, sacrifice, who served and paid the highest price.

Through countless acres occupied by these white tiers, the naked eye

Sees asymmetrical projection, ruler straight, in all directions,
Stretching outward distantly, as if into infinity;
Expressed in stone the human toll of bygone years, which mock the soul.

So let these symbols of man's past barbarity remain and last
Forever in our memory, to trust there will no longer be
A need for such displays again, to banish all the grief and pain
That these stones sadly represent, of human suffering, dark torment.

And if their future presence should result in world peace, then some good
Will have been wrought, and those who fell will have achieved in their farewell
A better victory than they thought they would secure. They, dying, sought
To end all war, so peace remained. For their sake, this should be attained.

TeeCee

Six-One-Seven Squadron. The Dam Busters.

Towards the gathering night they flew, this gallant band of airmen who
Would, by their exploits be recalled whenever tales were being told
Of bold courageous deeds by men, who came to serve their country when
The dark, grim war clouds cloaked our land with menace, grim, forbidding hand.

They set forth on this daunting mission with faith and trust in the decision
And belief in Boffins view that bombs would bounce, a hitherto
Untested theory, now applied, potentially a suicidal
Journey into the unknown, yet undeterred, continued on.

And so the legend then was born, how nineteen aircraft, one by one,
Left Scampton airfield in mid-May, to fly and find the dams that they
Were to destroy, and flood the plains below, and ultimately gain
Advantage in the fighting done through three long years since war began.

As they took to evening skies, attempting to achieve surprise,
They flew at almost zero feet, a stunning and astounding feat
Of airmanship, though in the dark, some paid the price of risk in stark
Realities of flight so low, colliding with the ground below.

But yet, undaunted, they flew on, and targeted by hostile guns,
Some fell to earth, not fated to complete their mission, see it through;
While nine did reached their destination, darkness shrouding observation,
Making difficult decisions, trying to bomb with precision.

Ignoring gunfire, smoke and flak, they held their course and, throttling back
Approached at the height specified, until through simple sight espied
The twin towers that set the distance, pressed on with complete persistence,
Pressing bomb release to climb out of harms way, and look behind.

The missile, true to boffin's word, skipped and bounced - it looked absurd
That something, ten tons, five feet long should, like pebble in a pond,
Behave in such a artless way, yet there it was, and in a spray
Of water, struck, the towers between, and sank just as was first foreseen.

Eruptions to a thousand feet; at first crews thought their task complete,
Yet no, more effort was required, and they bent to their task, inspired
Until, at last, they did achieve their aim, then, finally took their leave
For other targets yet to come, complete their mission, then go home.

And, as the legend tells us so, these men, these gallant fliers go
On bravely, guarantee success, yet at a cost which, nonetheless
Is that which airmen recognise, when, by armed conflict in the skies,
There may be sacrifice entailed, yet willingly they do prevail.

And now recalling their deeds then, we honour these brave men again,
These fliers, who, some, almost boys, took up the challenge, made the choice
To take that flight, despite the cost of fifty-three brave souls that lost
Their future when they ventured there, to do their duty in the air.

Some say that this is history, and yes, it is, we must agree,
Yet history's message is quite plain that in ignoring it again,
Then, once more young folk must arise and maybe make that sacrifice
That others had made in the past, But let us pray we've seen the last!

TeeCee

Soldier First – REME

Soldier first before all else, that is the REME way,
And there's a price – a tragic price – that some are called to pay.
It's not enough to use those skills as artisans to work
In maintenance and technicalities, and hope to shirk
The overriding reason why our soldiers pledge their all,
To fight, defending country and obeying duty's call.

And where the British Army serves, at home, or distantly,
Then REME soldiers will be there, and by necessity
Will fight as equals, help, assist to bear their comrade's load,
Share any deprivation or discomfort that affords.
And should they fall and ultimately be called on to pay
The highest price, then as always, that is the REME way.

TeeCee

Soldiers who Fight

Those who take perverse delight condemning our soldiers, who fight,
Should, perhaps take pause, reflect that all those of whom they object
Could be the ones that stand between them when they try to vent their spleen
And future dictatorial men who try by force to see again
That speech, opinions voiced contrary, would be silenced, and the very
Freedom that we hold so dear and take so much for granted here,
Would disappear without a trace, leaving all subdued, to face
A future where all thought is banned, and hopes dispersed as grains of sand.

A history book is all we need to instruct those who care to read
About the men from every age whose sole ambition was to wage
Destructive war, to conquer all, but were defeated by the call
To arms of peoples who placed high the freedom, that would be denied
Should they just meekly acquiesce to force, and try to make the best
Of slavery in heart and mind, no self-respect. To fate, resigned.
Condemned by liberal mindsets who had not the wit to see that through,
And only through a soldiers eyes we could resist those so despised.

So do not lightly criticise those who, from duty, place their lives
At our disposal, in belief that better things will grow, bequeathing
 Peace and freedom in our time, willing to defend if signs
Of dictatorial intent show. Therefore assure them that they know
We gladly give our full support to those brave lads who bravely fought
And even now, fight in the cause of peace and justice, for it does
Help see them through their darkest hours, aiding, strengthening their powers
Of high resolve with grit and nerve, to gain the victory they deserve.

TeeCee

Stand Easy

No need at last to turn out more than the usual 'five minutes before'
No final rub with yellow duster assembling for the morning muster,
Duties now are in the past it's time for you now to 'stand fast',
You did your time, you gave your best, and now you've more than earned your rest;
So sleep your sleep Old Soldier - Friend, contented, knowing in the end,
That all your friends will pause awhile and fondly think of you – and smile.

TeeCee

The Final Sunset

(To the tune of "The Last Post")

The time is here
To say farewell to yesteryear.
Thousands of boyhood memories are here,
But their history was engraved here, for three score years and ten,
Now sacrificed to progress and the march of time again,
But like old soldiers it never dies,
Just fading with the darkening skies,
Some misty eyes,
At the last, final Goodbye.

TeeCee

The Likely Lads

Bill and Jock were likely lads, who weren't averse to fun,
Especially if the opposite sex was there, to give them some.
It came about that, on the pull, their luck was in, and how!
A nurse apiece, in generous mood? The lads weren't ever slow
In taking up the offer made - the opportunity
To give the girls some useful tips, reproductively!

All went very well at first, progress was first class,
Stripped for action were our lads, bare from head to @*se.
When suddenly, a warning shout, "The Matron's on her way!"
And Phil and Jock then understood the meaning of the phrase,
'Coitus Interuptus - and they knew that they were done,
So swift withdrawal was required, in more ways than one!

Jock, through the window with one bound, he grasped the drainpipe there,
But in his haste misjudged his pace and all he grabbed was air!
The gravity of what he'd done was brought to his attention
As he plummeted some twenty feet - Oh, I'd forgot to mention
That the nurses lived on a third floor accommodation block,
A fact now really underlined by bruised and battered Jock!

At least he had escaped the trap, but Phil was still inside,
Desperately searching round the room for a place to hide.
A small wall locker he espied, it was his only chance
To save himself, or he would face the awful consequence
Of Matrons wrath, which in itself, you'd think was bad enough,

Made ten times worse as he was standing there, shivering in his buff!

Desperate situations need desperate measures, so
Phil squeezes in the locker, too small, but he'd to go
Into weird contortions, his limbs he had to bend
To fit inside, he finished up real close to his best friend!
And locked inside, he heard the voice of She who ruled supreme,
Berating Jock, who, through the open window heard her scream,

"Fornicating Weasel!" as he scuttled through the gloom,
Pale white thighs reflecting the light of silvery moon.
But luckily, she - satisfied that only one was there -
Departed, leaving Phil to tumble from his lair.
With creaks and groans, and aching bones, he vowed for evermore,
That if there was a next time, It would be on the Ground Floor!

TeeCee

A Soldiers Tale (21st Century Style

The soldier said, "I never thought,"as he faced the seething throng,
"That the pen was mightier than the sword,I couldn't be more wrong."
"I've got just five rounds in the mag, my body armour's duff,
My Family's living in a slum, I think I've had enough."

"That damned accountant with his pen, up in the treasury,
Is calculating where and when the next chop's going to be."
"If he and all his cronies there had served Queen and Country,
He'd sure think twice and wouldn't dare to use that pen so free."

"They send us out - in harms way, and haven't got a clue
What life is like, when day to day you know it could be YOU".
"They have no understanding of the words by which we live.
'Loyalty', 'Truth', 'Comradeship,' not 'Take, take, take,' but 'Give'."

"From University they go, onto a stepping stone, to
A sinecure, then a safe seat, no sweat, no effort ? - No!"
"Just a willingness to do as they are told , like sheep,
Rewards will surely then accrue, as up the scale they creep."

"And finally, they reach the top, the Ministries they prized,
Then, at all costs, avoid the chop, as their true worth is realized".
"But self delusion has its day, reality, no place.
They know they're right and others wrong, hard facts they will not face."

"Our troops have earned deserved renown of that there is no doubt,
But useless leaders let them down, and now they're getting out."
So don't expect things to improve the country is in tatters - but
Priorities are balance sheets, and nought else really matters".

"And it all comes down to just one fact, that all things have a cost,
And while accountants make the rules, HUMANITY IS LOST>

TeeCee

The Soldier

He never saw himself as brainy, in fact, "uni" was never his aim,
But then, common sense and intelligence were not necessarily the same.
He wanted to live life in practise, academia just didn't appeal,
Experience versus just theory, he fancied a life that was real.

But where to go to find this lifestyle? How would he find what he sought?
He looked at vocations with mounting impatience, but all his research came to nought.
Until watching the news in the evening, an item came, showing the feats
Of a squad of young soldiers in action, then he knew that his search was complete.

And now he had found what he wanted, a role of vitality, action,
A worthwhile career, that increasingly clearly would give him supreme satisfaction.
But then, as he pondered the various options of Corps or a Regiment's choice,
An item came on with news-changing views that paused him with still, warning voice.

These men who had fought for their country, risking life and limb, some having died
Were being abandoned and then persecuted by those on whom they had relied
To safeguard their interests and welfare in grateful, well-

deserved recognition,
Instead, being blighted by those parasites who belonged to the legal profession.

And then, in detecting that far from protecting their loyally brave fighting men,
Those who should have given them aid and support, betrayed them again and again,
So, with sad, heavy heart he knew that the risks were too great and were just not for him,
But what price a life for a servicemen now? The outlook must surely be grim!

TeeCee

The Uniformed Engineer

Seemingly, at casual glance, a typical British soldier stands
In readiness to carry out his duty, with the fears and doubts
Anticipated combat brings, when all the valued, precious things
By which his life is so defined are sharply focused in his mind.

But then, on further close inspection, there's a varied odd collection
Of the tool-chests, kits of parts which he must carry; written charts,
To aid his task, to give support to others who, engaged in fraught
Combat conditions must rely on expertise that he supplies.

This is an army engineer, a REME soldier, always near
And close at hand when something fails, with instant help when war assails
The fighting troops in forward line. Split seconds passing can define
That help, on which they must rely, and means that men could live or die.

This is a REME Craftsman's lot, and though he may be far from shot
And shell, his work can mark success or failure if, under duress
He falters in an urgent task, to give the help that others ask
For, in their time of urgent need, relying on the REME Creed.

The Creed that says it will provide, at all times, aid, and will abide
By that which when it first was formed, where all privations would be borne
To be at hand and share the plight, when needed, and prepare to fight
If urgent circumstances beckoned; "Soldier first, and Tradesman second".

So those who wish to join and fight for glory, kudos; wear the bright
Medallions of the regiments whose bold, historic past events
Add glamour to their daily lives, forget the REME; it relies
On quietly working, meeting needs of those performing front-line deeds.

But it is worthwhile to record that in all regiment's awards
Of battle honours so displayed as when in glittering parade,
The REME show no honours there, for since formation they have shared
A presence, fighting EVERY action, so they have the satisfaction
Of quietly knowing, if awarded, battle honours, so recorded
Might stretch so far as they unfurled to be the longest in the world!

TeeCee

Thoughts on being a Soldier

A soldier's life is his alone, he only volunteers to loan
It to his country for a while, to help secure our native isle
Against those who would see it fall, where, if the Nation's siren call
For strong, decisive action sounds then willingly he will be found
To step in line and ready to serve as required, seeing it through.

A soldier's life is based on trust in all whom he relies on, just
As do his comrades sharing danger, but those who also are a stranger
To the hazards of his task, who, safe at distant desks will ask
Him for commitment every day, knowing he might have to pay
A high price for his dedication, enduring peril and privation.

A soldier's life is shared with others, closer than his natural brothers,
For these are those who knew him well, shared his laughter and the hell
That might have been his daily lot, who stood four square in battle, fought
With courage and resolve with him, and loyally, through thick and thin,
Will utter, firm resolve did stay and faced what came, when in harm's way.

A soldier's life is understood by those who've served, but never could
Be recognised or learned by those who in civilian life can

choose
To please themselves if so inclined, where servicemen cannot decline
If ordered into danger, they must, by their code, accept, obey,
Regardless of their thoughts of why they may be called to fight and die.

A soldier's life is not a thing to be discarded, when looking
To prettify a balance sheet; so all those figures laid in neat
Accountant's books in Government ignore the real world, and those bent
On placing us in peril, who, unless dissuaded will see through
Our cost-priority blinkered chiefs, who risk all for fiscal beliefs.

Therefore, respect a soldier's life, it falls to us to stay the knife
Of those who would make easy gain by ignoring the steady drain
Of our defensive expertise, neglecting that which kept the peace.
An army, ready to defend this land of ours right to the end,
For history may repeat the time of that year, Nineteen Thirty Nine……

Three Statues

Along a beach of golden sand in northern France, three statues stand:
Commemorating soldiers who, long years before accomplished, through
Their exploits told in time of war, a place in history's folklore
Of courage, leadership and nerve, and dedication just to serve.

One statue recalls high command, the leader who conceived and planned
The battle soon to be contested, upon whom, lives of thousands rested.
Next, the man, bold, unafraid who, leading his elite brigade,
Advanced in face of hostile fire, this Highland Chief of Scottish Shires .

And finally, yet never least, an unassuming lad who ceased
To be a youth that fateful day when taking up his pipes to play,
He entered into legend there, as battle raged the highland airs
Refused to bow to conflict's pain he answered with the pipe's refrain.

These statues mark extraordinary men, who in their way do represent
All, each and every man that day, their duty too, their part to play
In yet another story of war's brutal cost, but then, above
It all, despite the cruel price of conflict, men of note will

rise.

And at Sword Beach in Normandy the statue of Montgomery,
The Brigadier, Lord Lovat, too, these leaders of the brave men who
Fought on that day - but up on high, in silhouette against the sky,
The figure of Bill Millin plays, a humble piper, showing the way.

TeeCee

Watching and Waiting

Your feet are so cold, your breath mistily shrouds
The window beside you, you gaze at the clouds
Scudding so swiftly on the face of the moon,
Watching and waiting for dawn to come soon.

You take a pace forward, into the chill
Of air that stings sharply, and an effort of will
Is needed to shoulder your rifle again,
Watching and waiting for night-time to wane.

Your beat's twenty paces, and then turn about,
Remember its 'left turn', then paces to count
Till right about turn, so you're facing your front,
Watching and waiting till your watch is spent.

The clock on the guardroom says twenty to four,
An hour or so later, it reads ten minutes more,
They say that time flies, but you take leave to doubt,
Watching and waiting for time to run out.

The bark of a fox hidden in the shadow,
At least he's got choices of places to go,
He's out on the prowl, slinks on his way,
Watching and waiting to leap on his prey.

The Orderly Officer's skulking around
So be on alert, keep your ear to the ground,
He's lurking close somewhere, without any doubt,
Watching and waiting to call the Guard out!

You look at the shrubs, growing over the way,

They're moving around, your eyes start to play
Tricks on your brain, blink, and then carry on,
Watching and waiting till your stag is done.

The grey streaks of morning appear in the East,
It seems it's a lifetime you've been on your feet,
You know that it's over - the sun's rising fast,
Watching and waiting is over at last!

TeeCee

Whither the Army now?

The ghosts are there, formed up in line, muskets shouldered, brassworks shine
And glint as guidons proudly fly, proclaiming glorious years gone by;
Recalling Monk and Marlborough too, who resonate in fame and who,
With Wellington engraved their names in history, and rightly claimed
The loyalty of those they led, and by their deeds ensured great dread
And fear to those whose thoughts aspired to subjugate Brittania's shires.

From Quebec's Heights, Sevastopol, Corunna, Alma; these are all
Names honoured by the regiments who fought these battles, and the men
Who gave their lives; are still recalled on Standards carried, still extolled
By those who proudly carry on traditions, which were set in stone,
Remembering the human cost of countless soldiers who were lost
In battles long ago, so we could live in peace, remaining free.

The British Army is unique. It gains its strength and proud mystique
From close bonds formed, as family, with fortitude and loyalty
Found far beyond the armies who fight for a price, as mercenaries do.

These families, whose deeds are writ large in our nation's own ambit,
Bear County names, identified and honoured with due pomp and pride,
While Special Services and Corps served selflessly these native shores.

But now, in this new, modern age, those in power seem not to gauge
The sacrifice and brave endeavour of those soldiers who would never
Calculate a balance sheet against the prospect of defeat
By ignorance and dereliction by mistaken, false conviction
That it is really pounds and pence that matter more than our defence,
These politicians, so naïve make bad decisions, misconceived.

Sole use of numbers is the key to all rules of accountancy,
But the great failing of this creed leads some to selfishness and greed
And in its gross, complete absence of thoughtfulness and common sense,
Takes no account of our real life, of human failings, fear and strife
That emanates from evil men who will triumph if we, again,
Are not prepared to spend to fight, defend the things we know are right.

A part-time army looks secure to those who will choose to ignore
How lessons of past times repeat, with victory snatched from defeat
Only by those who understood the logic of a strong and good
Defence Force that is highly trained, a fact that ought to be

explained
To politicians, who, divorced from real life, should be really forced
To read our recent history - to them, it seems, a mystery!

TeeCee

Winter

Winters here, yes, summer's gone, time to put the Long Johns on!
We're back to scraping off the frost, bemoaning plants that we've just lost
For not responding to the chill in time, and watching fuel bills
Climb ever upwards on the rise, while those who can, take to the skies
Seeking lands where warmth beguiles, most likely, the Canary Isles!

I think, I sometimes wish I was in some place warmer, just like Oz,
Although, out there it just ain't funny finding wild life in the dunny!
So, on reflection, I'll stay here, sod the lager, I'll drink beer,
Though warm, unlike the weather local, I take note of opinions vocal,
In extolling life down under, giving me some thoughts to ponder!

But let's return to the main theme, considering what many seem
To do, when icy winds prevail, up sticks and leg it, fly or sail
To pastures new for the duration, leaving this cold, glacial nation
Shivering, in spite of thermal clothing, braving the infernal
Grey, cold, damp and glacial mornings, weather changes without warning.

However, now I do recall when I was in the tropics, all

I wanted was some short respite from steamy sweaty days and nights
Where it was near impossible to cool down, lying in a pool
Of perspiration, longing for those cosy, happy days of yore,
When, wrapped in bedding, I would sit in cosy comfort in my pit!

So maybe, on mature reflection, there is no place we'll find perfection
In a climate exquisite, without some detrimental bit
To make us stop and think again that we, at least, don't have the pain
Of earthquakes, hurricanes and such that others have to bear so much.
Therefore, though perfect they appear - on second thoughts, I'll stay right here!

TeeCee

Army Wives

It is lately the fashion for ladies of passion to demand equal rights in their lives,
Yet the hardships they mention defy comprehension to our loyal long suffering wives.
These verbose dolly birds would find it absurd and most likely would go out on strike,
If faced with the things that that a service life brings to our ladies and families alike.

The strident appeals that we're hearing just deals with attaining some business career,
And the tasks of wife, mother, are somehow another role, therefore precluded, we hear.
So it seems that, at best, this should be addressed, and our ladies be given their due,
For when all's said and done, they are the ones who give our lads the will to thrive, too.

Who is it that, at the drop of a hat, finds their carefully planned life awry,
And suddenly find that their husband's in combat, while they must continue to try
To pursue life's normality, in the reality that there could be some bad news to come?
Yet they put it aside, take it all in their stride, uncomplaining, courageous, each one.

And while they're apart, who is facing the start of each day, minding family affairs,
Raising children alone, far from family and home, single-handedly dealing with cares

And the regular routine, and always the umpteen small things that occur in the day?
Valiantly coping and fervently hoping that her man will be not long away.

And those women who sneer, pursuing careers would do well to take note and take heed
Of these ladies who hold the heart and the soul of our soldiers who serve country's needs,
And never refute – they're as tough as old boots – the great contribution they make,
By giving their men the belief that they cope and succeed in whatever it takes.

And to those who've been there, done it all, had their share of the role of a military wife,
When times were much harder, separation much longer but never gave up on the life,
A special acclaim to you who became the example to all who have come
And followed your lead, and in turn, guaranteed the high standards which you had begun.

So then, chaps, raise your glasses to these lovely lasses who never signed on as you did,
And give them three cheers for the many long years that they willingly gave you, amid
Countless upheavals - married quarters, some evil, in places quite strange and exotic,
Where prolonged residence in surroundings intense could make less stable ladies neurotic!

TeeCee

At the Cenotaph

Yes, I saw them standing there with quiet, understated air,
But what a glorious sight they made, stepping smartly on parade!
For just one hour, or maybe two, the intervening years just flew
Away, and there they were again, ignoring ages aches and pains.

The medals gleamed and shone so bright, reflecting chill November light
As, shoulders back, they marched with pride, honouring their friends who died,
And old, familiar marches brought the memories back of those who fought
With them and fell, so very young, heroes all, with deeds unsung.

And, for those in recent times, far from home in foreign climes,
Too many died, again the flower of youth, sent thence by those in power;
For war was ever made by those who, sat in distant, lofty pose
Required the young to fight and die, with loved ones left to grieve and cry.

But that was e'er the soldiers lot, to battle on, however fraught
The circumstances that are found, and to obey, they're duty bound,
For honour, truth and loyalty are soldier's strengths for all

to see;
So, for the price that they might pay, we all must keep Remembrance Day.

TeeCee